THE ESSENCE OF INDIAN PHILOSOPHY

AN OVERVIEW

NAMAN KUMAR AGARWAL

Made with ♥ on the Notion Press Platform
www.notionpress.com

To the love of my life and my family.

You are my world.

Contents

Preface

Indian philosophy is an ancient and profound wellspring of wisdom that has shaped the spiritual and intellectual fabric of one of the world's oldest civilisations. This book, Unveiling the Wisdom: An Introduction to Indian Philosophy, aims to provide readers with a comprehensive and accessible overview of the critical ideas, schools of thought, and philosophical texts that have emerged from the Indian subcontinent over the millennia.

Drawing from orthodox and heterodox traditions, this book delves into the rich tapestry of Indian thought, exploring the timeless concepts of dharma, karma, and liberation and the diverse philosophical schools such as Samkhya, Yoga, Vedanta, Buddhism, and Jainism. By examining the historical and cultural contexts from which these ideas emerged and their enduring influence on global spirituality and culture, Unveiling the Wisdom offers a unique and enriching perspective on the essence of Indian philosophy.

Whether you are a spiritual seeker, an academic, or simply curious about the world's great philosophical traditions, this book invites you to discover the insights and inspiration emanating from the rich heritage of Indian thought. By exploring key concepts, texts, and thinkers, you will gain a deeper understanding of the multifaceted nature of Indian philosophy and its ongoing relevance to our modern lives. As you embark on this journey, you will be encouraged to reflect on the wisdom of Indian philosophy and perhaps even find ways to integrate its teachings into your own life.

CHAPTER ONE

Introduction to Indian Philosophy

The Richness and Diversity of Indian Philosophy

The ancient origins of Indian thought

Indian philosophy boasts a rich and diverse history, tracing its roots back thousands of years to the ancient civilisations that inhabited the Indian subcontinent. Its origins can be found in the timeless wisdom of the Vedic period (c. 1500-500 BCE), a time when the foundations of Indian culture, religion, and thought were laid. The Vedas, the oldest and most sacred texts of Hinduism, form the bedrock of Indian philosophy, encapsulating many ideas, rituals, and concepts that would shape India's spiritual and intellectual landscape for millennia.

As Indian thought evolved, it began to encompass a wide range of perspectives, from the metaphysical speculations of the Upanishads to the ethical and practical teachings of Buddhism and Jainism. These diverse traditions represented different paths to spiritual liberation and offered various world views and approaches to understanding the nature of reality. The richness and diversity of Indian philosophy can be attributed to its ability to embrace a multiplicity of perspectives while maintaining a core set of beliefs and values that have stood the test of time.

The significance of Indian philosophy in global intellectual history

The influence of Indian philosophy extends far beyond the borders of the Indian subcontinent, significantly impacting global intellectual history. The profound ideas and spiritual insights that emerged from Indian philosophical traditions have resonated with thinkers and seekers across cultures and eras, contributing to developing various schools of thought and enriching the global tapestry of human understanding.

One of the earliest examples of Indian philosophy's influence in the broader world can be seen in its interaction with ancient Greek thought during the Hellenistic period. Following Alexander the Great's conquests in the Indian subcontinent, a period of cultural exchange ensued. Greek philosophers, such as Pyrrho and Anaxarchus, encountered Indian thought and incorporated elements of it into their teachings. Pyrrho, the founder of Greek Skepticism, was said to have been influenced by the tenets of Indian philosophy, particularly by the ideas of non-attachment and the suspension of judgment.

Another significant impact of Indian philosophy on global intellectual history can be seen in the spread of Buddhism across Asia. The teachings of the Buddha, which originated in India, would go on to shape the religious and philosophical landscapes of China, Japan, Korea, and Southeast Asia, inspiring countless individuals to embark on their spiritual journeys and fostering the development of new schools of Buddhist thought.

In more recent times, Indian philosophy has continued to captivate the minds of Western intellectuals and spiritual seekers alike. During the 19th and 20th centuries, the works of prominent Indian thinkers, such as Swami Vivekananda, Sri Aurobindo, and Rabindranath Tagore, garnered widespread attention in the West, sparking a renewed interest in the wisdom of the East. This fascination with Indian philosophy contributed to various intellectual and spiritual movements, such as Transcendentalism, Theosophy, and the New Age movement, which drew inspiration from Indian thought.

Moreover, Indian philosophy has played a crucial role in developing modern psychology and the study of consciousness. The Yoga Sutras of Patanjali, an ancient Indian text outlining the principles and practices of yoga, has provided a framework for understanding the nature of the mind and the transformative potential of meditation. Pioneers in psychology, such as Carl Jung and William James, were deeply influenced by the insights of Indian philosophy, and their works have profoundly shaped our understanding of the human psyche.

Furthermore, Indian philosophy's emphasis on the interconnectedness of all beings and its focus on holistic well-being have resonated with contemporary concerns regarding environmental sustainability and personal growth. The principles of ahimsa (non-violence) and the recognition of the interconnected web of life have inspired modern environmental movements and informed ethical debates on our relationship with the natural world.

In addition to its impact on psychology, spirituality, and environmental ethics, Indian philosophy has also contributed to mathematics, linguistics, and logic. The development of the concept of zero, for instance, has its roots in ancient Indian mathematics, and its subsequent adoption by the Islamic and Western worlds has had far-reaching consequences for the advancement of science and technology. Similarly, the sophisticated grammatical and linguistic theories developed by Indian scholars, such as Panini and Bhartrihari, have provided valuable insights into the nature of language and its relation to thought.

In conclusion, the richness and diversity of Indian philosophy have not only shaped the spiritual and intellectual heritage of the Indian subcontinent. Still, they have also left an indelible mark on global intellectual history. The profound ideas and insights that have emerged from Indian thought continue to inspire and inform our understanding of the human condition. Their relevance endures as we navigate the challenges and opportunities of the modern world. By engaging with the wisdom of Indian philosophy, we can draw upon a vast reservoir of knowledge and inspiration, enriching our lives and contributing to the collective pursuit of wisdom, understanding, and spiritual growth.

As we delve deeper into the various schools of thought and philosophical traditions that constitute Indian philosophy, we will continue exploring its impact on various disciplines and cultural contexts. Through this journey, we will not only uncover the multifaceted nature of Indian thought but also discover the timeless wisdom and insights it has to offer.

By engaging with Indian philosophy, we can expand our horizons and challenge our preconceived notions, thereby fostering a deeper understanding of the world and our place within it. Indian philosophy offers a wealth of knowledge, wisdom, and practical guidance to inform and inspire us in our quest for self-discovery, personal growth, and spiritual awakening.

As we venture into the fascinating world of Indian philosophy, we invite you to approach its teachings with an open mind and a curious spirit, ready to embrace the rich and diverse ideas that have shaped the spiritual and intellectual fabric of one of the world's oldest civilisations. Through this exploration, we hope to foster a greater appreciation of the enduring wisdom of Indian philosophy and inspire you to reflect on its relevance in your own life, contributing to your journey of growth, understanding, and self-realisation.

By examining the various schools of thought and delving into the key concepts and texts that underpin Indian philosophy, we will uncover the profound ideas and spiritual insights that have been passed down through the ages. From the metaphysical speculations of the Upanishads to the ethical teachings of the Buddha, the wisdom of Indian philosophy offers a multitude of paths to self-discovery, inner peace, and spiritual liberation.

Throughout this exploration, we encourage you to engage with the teachings of Indian philosophy critically and thoughtfully, reflecting on their relevance to your own life and personal experiences. As you immerse yourself in the rich tapestry of Indian thought, you may find yourself inspired to embark on your spiritual journey, incorporating the timeless wisdom of Indian philosophy into your daily life and personal practice.

Ultimately, studying Indian philosophy is not merely an intellectual pursuit but also a transformative experience that can awaken our deepest capacities for compassion, insight, and self-awareness. By engaging with the teachings of Indian philosophy, we open ourselves to the possibility of profound personal and spiritual growth, enriching our lives and contributing to the well-being of all beings.

As we continue our journey through Indian philosophy, let us approach each new idea, concept, and tradition with curiosity, humility, and a genuine desire to learn, grow, and evolve. In doing so, we not only honour the rich intellectual heritage of the Indian subcontinent but also contribute to the ongoing dialogue between cultures, disciplines, and spiritual traditions, fostering a deeper understanding of our shared human experience.

By exploring Indian philosophy's diverse schools of thought, we can gain valuable insights into the nature of reality, the human mind, and the meaning of life. From the Vedas' teachings to the Buddha's profound insights, Indian philosophy provides knowledge and wisdom that can illuminate our path towards self-realisation, inner peace, and spiritual liberation.

As we embark on this journey together, let us remember that studying Indian philosophy is not an end but a means to facilitate our personal and spiritual growth. Through reflection, contemplation, and practical application, the timeless wisdom of Indian philosophy can become a living reality in our own lives, guiding us towards greater understanding, compassion, and self-awareness.

The Historical Context of Indian Philosophy

The Indus Valley Civilization and its influence

The Indus Valley Civilisation, one of the world's earliest urban civilisations, flourished between 2600 and 1900 BCE in the northwestern region of the Indian subcontinent. Although the script used by the Indus Valley Civilization remains undeciphered, archaeological evidence suggests that this highly advanced civilisation had a well-developed social structure, trade networks, and religious practices. While it is difficult to ascertain the specific influence of the Indus Valley Civilization on the development of Indian philosophy, some scholars argue that certain aspects of Hinduism, such as the worship of a mother goddess and the practice of yoga, may have their roots in this ancient civilisation.

The Vedic Period and the emergence of philosophical thought

The Vedic Period (c. 1500-500 BCE) marked a significant turning point in the history of Indian thought, with the composition of the Vedas, the oldest and most sacred texts of Hinduism. The Vedas, consisting of the Rigveda, Samaveda, Yajurveda, and Atharvaveda, is a collection of hymns, prayers, and ritual instructions that form the foundation of Indian religious and philosophical thought.

The earliest philosophical ideas can be found in Rigveda, which contains hymns that speculate on the nature of the cosmos, the gods, and the creation of the universe. The development of Indian philosophical thought continued with the emergence of the Upanishads, the final and most important part of Vedic literature. The Upanishads shifted the focus from ritualistic practices to introspective and metaphysical speculation, addressing profound questions about the nature of reality, the self, and the ultimate goal of human existence.

The development of orthodox and heterodox schools

As Indian philosophy evolved, it began diversifying into orthodox (astika) and heterodox (nastika) schools. The orthodox schools accepted the authority of the Vedas and included six major systems: Samkhya, Yoga, Nyaya, Vaisheshika, Mimamsa, and Vedanta. Each of these schools developed its distinctive philosophy, methodologies, and practices while still adhering to the core principles of Vedic thought.

- **Samkhya:** This dualist philosophical system posits the existence of two fundamental realities: Purusha (consciousness) and Prakriti (matter). It provides a detailed analysis of the evolution of the universe and the process of liberation through the discrimination between Purusha and Prakriti.
- **Yoga:** Yoga, closely related to Samkhya, focuses on the practical aspects of spiritual development through a systematic approach to meditation, ethical conduct, and physical practices. The Yoga Sutras of Patanjali, an essential text in this tradition, outlines the eightfold path of yoga (Ashtanga Yoga) to achieve spiritual liberation.
- **Nyaya:** The Nyaya school is primarily concerned with logic, epistemology, and the rules of debate. It systematically analyses the nature of knowledge, perception, inference, and how valid knowledge can be acquired.
- **Vaisheshika:** This atomistic school of thought posits that the universe is composed of indivisible, eternal atoms (paramanus) that combine to form complex objects. Vaisheshika emphasises the classification and analysis of the material world, offering a detailed ontology and a causal theory of how the world functions.
- **Mimamsa:** The Mimamsa school focuses on interpreting and analysing the ritual aspects of the Vedas. It is primarily

concerned with the proper performance of rituals and attaining their results, asserting that the proper performance of Vedic rituals leads to desirable outcomes in this life and the afterlife.

- **Vedanta:** This school represents the culmination of Indian philosophical thought, focusing on the interpretation of the Upanishads and the nature of ultimate reality. Vedanta comprises several sub-schools, such as Advaita (non-dualism), Vishishtadvaita (qualified non-dualism), and Dvaita (dualism), each with its distinct philosophical positions regarding the relationship between the individual self (atman), the ultimate reality (Brahman), and the nature of spiritual liberation (moksha).

The heterodox schools, on the other hand, rejected the authority of the Vedas and developed their philosophical systems. The two major heterodox traditions are Buddhism and Jainism:

- **Buddhism:** Founded by Siddhartha Gautama, who became the Buddha, this tradition emphasises the principles of the Four Noble Truths and the Eightfold Path to overcome suffering and achieve enlightenment. Buddhism further diversified into various schools, such as Theravada, Mahayana, and Vajrayana, each with its interpretation of the Buddha's teachings.
- Jainism: Established by Mahavira, the 24th and last Tirthankara, Jainism stresses the principles of non-violence (ahimsa), non-absolutism (anekantavada), and non-possessiveness (aparigraha) as the path to spiritual liberation. Jainism's Emphasis on non-violence and strict asceticism has significantly impacted Indian culture, ethics, and religious practices.

The impact of foreign invasions and cultural exchanges

Throughout history, Indian philosophy has been influenced by foreign invasions and cultural exchanges. One of the most significant instances was during the Hellenistic period, following Alexander the Great's conquests in the Indian subcontinent. This period saw an exchange of ideas between Greek and Indian philosophers, leading to the incorporation of Indian thought into Greek philosophy, as evident in the works of Pyrrho and Anaxarchus.

The Mauryan Empire (c. 321-185 BCE) saw the rise of the Buddhist and Jain traditions, further contributing to the diversification of Indian philosophical thought. The influence of Buddhism expanded beyond India, spreading to China, Japan, Korea, and Southeast Asia, where it became a significant force in shaping their religious and philosophical landscapes.

During the Gupta Empire (c. 320-550 CE), Indian philosophy witnessed a period of consolidation and resurgence. The Vedanta school, in particular, reached its zenith under the guidance of the philosopher Adi Shankara, who formulated the Advaita Vedanta system. At the same time, Nalanda University, an ancient learning centre, attracted scholars from across the Indian subcontinent and beyond, fostering the exchange of ideas and the development of new philosophical insights.

The Islamic conquests in India (c. 12th-16th centuries) introduced new cultural and intellectual influences, including translating Indian philosophical texts into Persian and Arabic. During the Mughal Empire (c. 1526-1858), India experienced a synthesis of Islamic and Hindu thought, which led to the emergence of the Bhakti movement and the Sufi tradition, emphasising devotion and spiritual experience as the path to divine union.

The arrival of European colonial powers, particularly the British, in the 18th and 19th centuries brought Western philosophical ideas to India and sparked a renewed interest in Indian philosophy among Western scholars. This period also witnessed the emergence of modern Indian thinkers, such as Swami Vivekananda, Sri Aurobindo, and Rabindranath Tagore, who sought to reinterpret and reinvigorate Indian philosophical thought in the context of the challenges posed by modernity and colonialism.

In conclusion, the historical context of Indian philosophy is characterised by a rich tapestry of diverse intellectual traditions, cultural influences, and historical developments. From the enigmatic beginnings of the Indus Valley Civilization to the complex interplay of orthodox and heterodox schools during the Vedic Period, and from the impact of foreign invasions to the ongoing dialogue with Western philosophy, Indian thought has continually evolved and adapted to its ever-changing circumstances.

This dynamic history has given rise to a wealth of philosophical ideas and insights that have not only shaped the spiritual and intellectual fabric of the Indian subcontinent but have also left an indelible mark on global intellectual history. The enduring relevance and richness of Indian philosophy can be attributed, in part, to its ability to assimilate new ideas and respond to the challenges of different historical periods while remaining grounded in its ancient wisdom.

As we continue to explore the diverse schools of thought and philosophical traditions that constitute Indian philosophy, it is essential to appreciate the historical context that has shaped their development. By understanding the historical roots and cultural influences of Indian philosophical thought, we can gain a deeper appreciation for its complexity, richness, and enduring relevance, both within the Indian subcontinent and beyond.

In the following chapters, we will delve further into the key concepts, ideas, and thinkers of each major school of Indian philosophy, examining their historical development, philosophical foundations, and practical applications. Through this exploration, we aim to provide a comprehensive overview of the multifaceted world of Indian philosophical thought, shedding light on its enduring wisdom and ongoing relevance in our contemporary global society.

The Cultural Roots of Indian Philosophy

The role of religion and spirituality in shaping Indian thought

Religion and spirituality have shaped Indian thought and culture throughout history. Indian philosophy is deeply intertwined with the various religious traditions that have emerged in the region, including Hinduism, Buddhism, Jainism, and Sikhism. These religious traditions have been the primary vehicles for transmitting philosophical ideas and fostering intellectual inquiry, providing a rich and diverse foundation for developing Indian philosophical thought.

Hinduism, India's oldest and most widespread religious tradition, has significantly shaped Indian philosophy. The Vedas and the Upanishads, which form the basis of Hindu religious thought, are replete with profound philosophical insights and questions regarding the nature of reality, the self, and the ultimate purpose of human life. Various Hindu philosophy schools, such as Samkhya, Yoga, and Vedanta, have emerged from this foundational Vedic tradition, further elaborating on these ideas and developing their unique perspectives on the nature of existence, consciousness, and spiritual liberation.

Buddhism and Jainism, two major heterodox traditions in India, have also played a crucial role in the evolution of Indian philosophical thought. Both traditions, which originated around the same time in the 6th century BCE, rejected the authority of the Vedas and developed their distinct philosophical systems. Buddhism, emphasising the Four Noble Truths and the Eightfold Path, offers a comprehensive framework for understanding the nature of suffering and the path to enlightenment. Jainism, focusing on non-violence, non-absolutism, and non-possessiveness, provides a unique ethical and metaphysical perspective on the nature of reality and the path to spiritual liberation.

The role of religion and spirituality in shaping Indian thought is not limited to these major traditions. Other religious and spiritual movements, such as the Bhakti movement and Sufism, have also contributed to the development of Indian philosophy, emphasising the importance of devotion, mysticism, and direct experience of the divine as a means of spiritual growth.

India's close relationship between religion and philosophy has resulted in a unique cultural landscape where philosophical ideas are often expressed through religious texts, rituals, and practices. This interplay between religion and philosophy has fostered a holistic approach to understanding the human condition. Intellectual inquiry and spiritual experience are complementary and integral aspects of the quest for truth and self-realisation.

The interplay between philosophical ideas and social structures

Indian philosophy has not only been influenced by religion and spirituality but has also been deeply intertwined with the social and political structures of Indian society. The caste system, a hierarchical social structure that has existed in India for millennia, has played a significant role in shaping the development and dissemination of philosophical ideas.

The Brahmin caste, traditionally responsible for religious and intellectual pursuits, has historically been at the forefront of the development of Indian philosophy. As custodians of the sacred Vedas and other religious texts, Brahmins have been instrumental in preserving and transmitting India's philosophical heritage. However, this close association between the Brahmin caste and the intellectual sphere has also led to the exclusion and marginalisation of other social groups, which has, in turn, influenced the development of Indian philosophical thought.

The emergence of heterodox schools like Buddhism and Jainism can be a response to this exclusionary social structure. These traditions rejected the authority of the Vedas and the caste system and provided alternative philosophical frameworks that were more inclusive and accessible to a broader range of social groups. Similarly, the Bhakti movement and Sikhism emphasised the importance of devotion and spiritual equality, transcending the social boundaries imposed by the caste system.

The relationship between Indian philosophy and social structures is also evident in how philosophical ideas have influenced the development of social norms, ethical principles, and legal systems. For instance, dharma, a central theme in Hindu philosophy, has provided a basis for understanding individuals' moral obligations and duties within their social roles and relationships. Likewise, the principles of ahimsa (non-violence) and anekantavada (non-absolutism) in Jainism have significantly impacted the ethical and social values of Indian society.

Indian philosophy has also been closely associated with political thought and governance, as seen in the classic treatise on statecraft, the Arthashastra, written by the ancient Indian scholar Kautilya. The Arthashastra, which integrates principles from various Indian philosophical traditions, provides a comprehensive framework for understanding the state's nature, the rulers' responsibilities, and the importance of ethical conduct in governance.

The influence of language and literature on Indian philosophy

Language and literature have been vital to developing and transmitting Indian philosophical thought. Sanskrit, the classical language of India, has been the primary medium for expressing and preserving Indian philosophical ideas. The rich and complex nature of the Sanskrit language, with its vast vocabulary and precise grammatical rules, has allowed for nuanced expression and intricate philosophical analysis.

The influence of language on Indian philosophy is evident in the extensive use of poetry, metaphor, and allegory to convey philosophical concepts and insights. The use of these literary devices has not only made philosophical ideas more accessible and engaging. Still, it has also allowed for exploring complex themes and ideas through creative and imaginative means. For instance, the Bhagavad Gita, a central text in the Hindu tradition, uses the metaphor of a conversation between the warrior-prince Arjuna and the god Krishna on the battlefield to explore deep philosophical questions regarding duty, action, and the nature of the self.

Indian literature has also been a fertile ground for expressing and developing philosophical ideas, with numerous literary works integrating philosophical themes and concepts into their narratives. The great Indian epics, the Mahabharata and the Ramayana provide a rich tapestry of mythological and historical narratives and serve as vehicles for exploring philosophical and ethical issues.

Classical Indian drama, as exemplified in the works of the playwright Kalidasa, also integrates philosophical themes and ideas, using the medium of theatre to explore the complexities of human emotions, relationships, and the nature of existence. Similarly, the vast body of Indian poetry, from the devotional verses of the Bhakti poets to the philosophical musings of the mystic Kabir, reflects the profound influence of Indian philosophical thought on the literary and cultural landscape of the Indian subcontinent.

In conclusion, the cultural roots of Indian philosophy are deeply intertwined with the religious, social, and linguistic traditions of the Indian subcontinent. The role of religion and spirituality in shaping Indian thought has fostered a rich and diverse foundation for the development of philosophical ideas and insights. The interplay between philosophical ideas and social structures has shaped the development of ethical norms, legal systems, and political thought in India, reflecting the close relationship between intellectual inquiry and societal organisation.

The influence of language and literature on Indian philosophy highlights the importance of creative expression and imaginative exploration in pursuing philosophical understanding. Through poetry, metaphor, allegory, and other literary devices, Indian philosophical ideas have been accessible, engaging, and relevant to countless individuals' lives.

By understanding the cultural roots of Indian philosophy, we can better appreciate the richness and diversity of this intellectual tradition and its enduring relevance in our contemporary global society. As we continue our exploration of the various schools of thought and philosophical traditions that constitute Indian philosophy, we will see how these cultural influences have shaped the development of profound and timeless ideas, providing us with a unique lens through which to view the human condition and the nature of reality.

The Philosophical Inquiry in Indian Thought

The quest for truth and self-realisation

At the heart of Indian philosophical inquiry lies the quest for truth and self-realisation. The diverse schools of thought that make up Indian philosophy share a common goal: understanding the nature of reality, the self, and the ultimate purpose of human existence. This pursuit of truth is often expressed as a spiritual journey, a path to enlightenment or liberation from the cycle of birth and death, known as samsara.

In Indian thought, the quest for truth is not seen as a purely intellectual endeavour but as a holistic process that integrates knowledge, experience, and ethical conduct. The various philosophical systems offer different paths to self-realisation, emphasising aspects of human experiences, such as knowledge, devotion, action, and contemplation.

For example, the Advaita Vedanta school of Hindu philosophy teaches that the ultimate truth is the non-dual nature of reality. The individual self (atman) and the ultimate reality (Brahman) are the same. This realisation can be attained through the cultivation of spiritual knowledge, meditation practice, and a qualified teacher's guidance.

Similarly, the Buddhist tradition teaches that the path to enlightenment involves the cultivation of wisdom, ethical conduct, and mental discipline, as outlined in the Eightfold Path. The Buddhist concept of anatta (no-self) challenges the notion of a permanent, unchanging self. It emphasises the importance of understanding the interdependent nature of all phenomena to attain liberation from suffering.

The quest for truth and self-realisation in Indian thought has also led to the development of a rich and diverse array of spiritual practices, ranging from meditation and yoga to devotional rituals and asceticism. These practices are designed to cultivate the qualities and insights necessary for spiritual growth, enabling individuals to experience the truths of the various philosophical systems directly.

The exploration of metaphysics, epistemology, ethics, and aesthetics

Indian philosophy is characterised by its rigorous exploration of metaphysics, epistemology, ethics, and aesthetics. These four branches of philosophical inquiry provide a comprehensive framework for understanding the nature of reality, the sources and limits of knowledge, the principles of moral action, and the relationship between beauty and truth.

Metaphysics, the study of the nature of reality, is a central theme in Indian philosophical thought. Various schools of Indian philosophy have developed intricate metaphysical systems that seek to explain the nature of existence, the relationship between the self and the universe, and the ultimate nature of reality. For instance, the Samkhya school posits a dualistic metaphysical framework in which Prakriti (matter) and purusha (consciousness) are the fundamental principles of reality. In contrast, the Advaita Vedanta school asserts the non-dual nature of reality, where the ultimate truth is the oneness of atman (individual self) and Brahman (ultimate reality).

Epistemology, the study of knowledge, is another key aspect of Indian philosophical inquiry. Indian philosophers have extensively debated the nature of knowledge, the sources of valid knowledge (pramanas), and the criteria for determining the truth. The various schools of Indian thought recognise different pramanas, such as perception, inference, analogy, and testimony, as valid means of acquiring knowledge. The Nyaya school, in particular, has developed a sophisticated epistemological framework that emphasises the importance of logic, argumentation, and empirical evidence in establishing the truth.

Ethics, the study of moral principles and values, is closely intertwined with the metaphysical and epistemological aspects of Indian philosophy. The concept of dharma, which can be understood as the moral and ethical order of the universe, is central to Indian ethical thought. The various schools of Indian philosophy have developed detailed ethical theories that address questions related to individual and social conduct, moral responsibility, and the path to spiritual liberation. For instance, the Karma-Yoga path in the Bhagavad Gita emphasises the importance of selfless action, performed without attachment to the fruits of one's actions, as a means of realising one's true nature.

Aesthetics, the study of beauty and artistic expression, is another important aspect of Indian philosophical inquiry. Indian philosophers have explored the nature of beauty, the relationship between art and reality, and the role of artistic expression in the pursuit of truth and self-realisation. The concept of rasa, which refers to the emotional essence or aesthetic experience evoked by a work of art, is central to Indian aesthetic theory. Indian thinkers such as the ancient theorist Bharata and the medieval philosopher Abhinavagupta have developed sophisticated rasa theories, emphasising the transformative power of art and its capacity to convey profound truths and insights.

The emphasis on logical reasoning, debate, and contemplation

Indian philosophy is characterised by its emphasis on logical reasoning, debate, and contemplation as essential tools for the pursuit of truth and self-realisation. The various schools of Indian thought have developed intricate systems of logic and argumentation that have been used to analyse and refine philosophical concepts, resolve disputes, and defend their respective positions. The Nyaya and Vaisheshika schools, in particular, have significantly contributed to developing Indian logic and epistemology, providing a rigorous framework for philosophical inquiry.

Debate and dialogue have been central to the Indian philosophical tradition, fostering a dynamic exchange of ideas and promoting a spirit of intellectual inquiry and critical thinking. Traditional Indian debates, known as shastrartha, were often held in public forums, where scholars from different schools would engage in rigorous discussions and disputes to establish the validity of their positions. These debates were conducted according to strict rules of argumentation and etiquette, and success was considered a mark of intellectual prowess and mastery of one's discipline.

Contemplation, meditation, and reflection have also been crucial in Indian philosophical inquiry. The practice of dhyana (meditation) is considered an essential means of cultivating the concentration, insight, and direct experiential knowledge necessary for attaining truth and self-realisation. Various schools of Indian philosophy have developed specific meditation techniques and practices designed to facilitate the direct experience of the truths expounded in their respective systems.

In summary, the philosophical inquiry in Indian thought is marked by a relentless quest for truth and self-realisation, a comprehensive exploration of metaphysics, epistemology, ethics, and aesthetics, and a strong emphasis on logical reasoning, debate, and contemplation. The richness and diversity of Indian philosophical thought can be attributed to the interplay between these various elements, providing a holistic framework for understanding the nature of reality, the self, and the ultimate purpose of human existence.

Throughout its long history, Indian philosophy has demonstrated a remarkable capacity for innovation, adaptation, and synthesis, responding to the challenges and questions posed by different historical and cultural contexts. The Indian philosophical tradition has not only enriched the intellectual and spiritual heritage of the Indian subcontinent. Still, it has also significantly contributed to global philosophical thought, offering a wealth of insights and perspectives that continue to inspire and challenge us today.

As we delve deeper into the various schools of thought and philosophical systems that constitute Indian philosophy, we will see how this rich and diverse tradition has shaped the development of profound and timeless ideas, providing us with a unique lens through which to view the human condition and the nature of reality. The philosophical inquiry in Indian thought represents an enduring testament to the power of human reason, imagination, and spiritual aspiration in pursuing truth, wisdom, and self-realisation.

The Unique Features of Indian Philosophy

The synthesis of rationality and mysticism

One of the unique features of Indian philosophy is its synthesis of rationality and mysticism. Indian thought has always sought to balance the analytical rigour of logical reasoning and the intuitive insights of mystical experience. This synthesis can be seen in how Indian philosophy integrates metaphysics, epistemology, ethics, and aesthetics with spiritual practices such as meditation, yoga, and devotional worship.

This blend of rationality and mysticism is evident in the teachings of various schools of Indian philosophy. For instance, the Advaita Vedanta school combines logical reasoning and scriptural analysis with the contemplative practices of meditation and self-inquiry to realise reality's non-dual nature. Similarly, the Buddhist tradition combines rigorous philosophical analysis with mindfulness and meditation to cultivate wisdom, compassion, and inner transformation.

The synthesis of rationality and mysticism in Indian philosophy underscores the holistic nature of Indian thought, which seeks to engage the whole human being—intellect, emotion, and spirit—in pursuing truth and self-realisation.

The interconnectedness of diverse philosophical schools

Another unique feature of Indian philosophy is the interconnectedness of its diverse philosophical schools. Despite the wide range of perspectives and doctrines in the Indian philosophical tradition, there is remarkable dialogue, cross-fertilisation, and mutual influence among the various schools of thought. This interconnectedness is evident in the way different philosophical systems build upon, refine, and critique the ideas of their predecessors and contemporaries, leading to the development of a rich and dynamic intellectual tradition.

This spirit of dialogue and debate among the diverse schools of Indian philosophy is exemplified by the distinction between astika and nastika philosophies. Astika philosophies, such as the six orthodox schools of Hindu thought, accept the Vedas' authority and share common metaphysical and epistemological assumptions. In contrast, nastika philosophies, such as Buddhism and Jainism, reject the authority of the Vedas and offer alternative perspectives on the nature of reality and the path to spiritual liberation.

Despite these differences, the various astika and nastika schools have engaged in fruitful exchanges of ideas and critiques, contributing to the refinement and evolution of Indian philosophical thought. This interconnectedness fosters a spirit of intellectual openness and inquiry that allows Indian philosophy to explore various perspectives and insights while maintaining a coherent and integrated understanding of the human quest for truth and self-realisation.

The adaptability and resilience of Indian thought

The adaptability and resilience of Indian thought is other unique feature of Indian philosophy. Throughout its long history, Indian philosophy has demonstrated a remarkable capacity for innovation, synthesis, and adaptation, responding to the challenges and questions posed by different historical and cultural contexts. This adaptability has allowed Indian philosophy to survive and thrive in political upheavals, foreign invasions, and cultural exchanges, incorporating new ideas and perspectives while preserving its core insights and values.

For instance, the encounter between Indian thought and Hellenistic philosophy following the conquests of Alexander the Great led to the development of Greco-Buddhist art and the fusion of Greek and Indian ideas in the Gandhara school of art. Similarly, the interaction between Indian philosophy and Islamic thought during the medieval period enriched both traditions, resulting in new philosophical systems such as the Sufi-influenced Kashmir Shaivism and the Islamic-inspired syncretism of the Bhakti movement.

The adaptability and resilience of Indian thought can also be seen in how Indian philosophy has engaged with modernity and the challenges posed by science, technology, and globalisation. Indian philosophers and thinkers such as Swami Vivekananda, Sri Aurobindo, and Mahatma Gandhi have sought to reinterpret and reformulate the insights of Indian philosophy in the light of contemporary challenges, offering new perspectives on spirituality, ethics, and social change that remain relevant and inspiring today.

The focus on experiential knowledge and spiritual transformation

One of the most distinctive features of Indian philosophy is its focus on experiential knowledge and spiritual transformation. Unlike many Western philosophical traditions, which emphasise theoretical knowledge and abstract reasoning, Indian philosophy strongly emphasises direct, personal experience to attain wisdom, self-realisation, and spiritual liberation.

This focus on experiential knowledge can be seen in the way Indian philosophy integrates meditation, yoga, and other contemplative practices with its theoretical and doctrinal teachings. These practices aim not merely to acquire an intellectual understanding or develop mental faculties but to transform one's consciousness, cultivate inner wisdom, and ultimately realise the true nature of reality and the self.

For instance, in the Yoga Sutras of Patanjali, the practice of yoga is presented as an eightfold path that encompasses ethical disciplines, physical postures, breath control, and meditation, all of which are aimed at cultivating deep concentration, inner stillness, and ultimately, the realisation of one's true nature. Similarly, in the Buddhist tradition, practising mindfulness and meditation is central to cultivating insight, compassion, and inner transformation, leading to enlightenment and the cessation of suffering.

The focus on experiential knowledge and spiritual transformation in Indian philosophy underscores the practical, transformative nature of Indian thought. Rather than simply providing abstract theories or speculative metaphysics, Indian philosophy offers a holistic framework for cultivating wisdom, self-realisation, and spiritual liberation that encompasses human life's intellectual, ethical, and spiritual dimensions. This emphasis on experiential knowledge and inner transformation sets Indian philosophy apart from many other philosophical traditions and speaks to the enduring relevance and appeal of Indian thought in our contemporary world.

In conclusion, the unique features of Indian philosophy, such as the synthesis of rationality and mysticism, the interconnectedness of diverse philosophical schools, the adaptability and resilience of Indian thought, and the focus on experiential knowledge and spiritual transformation, make it a rich and fascinating intellectual tradition that continues to inspire and challenge us today. By exploring the wealth of insights and perspectives offered by Indian philosophy, we can deepen our understanding of the human condition, the nature of reality, and our ultimate purpose, while enriching our intellectual and spiritual horizons.

The Relevance of Indian Philosophy in Today's World

The resurgence of interest in Indian philosophy

In recent years, there has been a resurgence of interest in Indian philosophy, both in India and worldwide. This renewed interest can be attributed to several factors, including the growing recognition of the value of non-Western intellectual traditions, the search for alternative perspectives on spirituality and human development, and the increasing interconnectedness of our globalised world.

The resurgence of interest in Indian philosophy is evident in the growing number of academic programs, research initiatives, and publications devoted to studying Indian thought. Many universities and institutions worldwide now offer courses, degrees, and research programs in Indian philosophy, reflecting the recognition of its intellectual and cultural significance. Furthermore, the works of classical Indian philosophers and thinkers are being translated, studied, and critically engaged with by scholars from various disciplinary backgrounds, leading to a more inclusive and diverse global philosophical discourse.

At the same time, Indian philosophy is also finding a wider audience among the general public, as people from all walks of life seek to explore its rich insights and perspectives on the human condition, the nature of reality, and the path to spiritual fulfilment. This growing interest in Indian philosophy is reflected in the popularity of books, lectures, workshops, and online resources that make the teachings of Indian thought accessible and relevant to a contemporary audience. Many people are turning to Indian philosophy for guidance on personal growth, stress reduction, and the cultivation of mental and emotional well-being, as well as for insights into the ethical, social, and environmental challenges of our times.

The applicability of ancient wisdom to modern challenges

One of the reasons for the resurgence of interest in Indian philosophy is the recognition that its ancient wisdom can offer valuable insights and guidance for addressing the complex challenges of our modern world. Despite the vast differences in historical and cultural context, the teachings of Indian philosophy remain relevant and applicable to the issues and concerns that confront us today, including questions of ethics, social justice, environmental sustainability, and personal fulfilment.

For example, the principle of ahimsa or nonviolence, central to the ethical teachings of Jainism, Buddhism, and Hinduism, offers a powerful and timely message for a world grappling with the devastating consequences of war, terrorism, and social conflict. By promoting a culture of peace, compassion, and mutual understanding, the principle of ahimsa can serve as a foundation for a more just, harmonious, and sustainable world.

Similarly, the concept of dharma or duty, which is central to the ethical teachings of Hinduism and Buddhism, provides a framework for understanding individuals' responsibilities and obligations towards themselves, their families, their communities, and the larger society. This emphasis on duty and responsibility can offer guidance for addressing the complex ethical challenges we face in our personal and professional lives and for fostering a sense of civic engagement, social responsibility, and global citizenship.

In environmental sustainability, the holistic worldview of Indian philosophy, which recognises the interconnectedness of all living beings and the natural world, offers a compelling alternative to the reductionist and mechanistic perspectives that have dominated Western thought. By emphasising the intrinsic value and interdependence of all life forms, Indian philosophy can help cultivate a deeper sense of ecological awareness and responsibility and inspire innovative solutions to the environmental crises that threaten our planet.

On a personal level, the teachings of Indian philosophy on self-realisation, mindfulness, and inner transformation can offer valuable guidance for those seeking to cultivate a more balanced, fulfilling, and meaningful life. In a world characterised by stress, anxiety, and the relentless pursuit of material success, the insights of Indian philosophy can help us to reconnect with our inner selves, find peace and contentment in the present moment, and cultivate a deeper sense of purpose and well-being.

The role of Indian thought in fostering intercultural understanding and dialogue

Another important dimension of the relevance of Indian philosophy in today's world is its potential to foster intercultural understanding and dialogue. As our world becomes increasingly interconnected and interdependent, there is a growing need for meaningful engagement between different cultures, traditions, and worldviews. By exploring and appreciating the rich intellectual and spiritual heritage of Indian philosophy, we can enrich our understanding of the human condition and create a foundation for greater mutual respect, empathy, and cooperation between different cultures and societies.

One way in which Indian philosophy can contribute to intercultural understanding and dialogue is by offering alternative perspectives and insights that challenge and complement Western intellectual traditions. For instance, the emphasis on experiential knowledge, inner transformation, and spiritual liberation in Indian thought provides a valuable counterpoint to Western philosophy's rationalist, materialist, and individualist tendencies. By engaging with Indian philosophy, Western thinkers and scholars can broaden their intellectual horizons, question their assumptions and biases, and develop a more inclusive and pluralistic understanding of reality.

Furthermore, the diversity and pluralism that characterises Indian philosophy can serve as a model for engaging with other intellectual traditions and cultures in a spirit of openness, curiosity, and mutual learning. As we have seen, Indian philosophy encompasses a wide range of schools, doctrines, and perspectives, reflecting a long tradition of intellectual debate, dialogue, and synthesis. This openness to different ideas and viewpoints and the willingness to engage in critical reflection and self-examination can inspire us to approach other cultural and intellectual traditions with a similar spirit of humility, curiosity, and respect.

Moreover, the teachings of Indian philosophy on topics such as compassion, tolerance, and nonviolence can provide a valuable ethical foundation for promoting intercultural dialogue and understanding. By emphasising the shared values and aspirations that unite us as human beings, Indian philosophy can help to bridge the cultural, religious, and ideological divides that often fuel conflict and misunderstanding. By fostering a spirit of empathy, respect, and mutual learning, Indian philosophy can contribute to creating a more inclusive, harmonious, and peaceful world.

In conclusion, the relevance of Indian philosophy in today's world is evident in the growing interest in its teachings, the applicability of its ancient wisdom to modern challenges, and its potential to foster intercultural understanding and dialogue. By engaging with the rich intellectual and spiritual heritage of Indian thought, we can deepen our understanding of the human condition and contribute to creating a more just, sustainable, and harmonious world. As we continue to explore and appreciate the insights and perspectives offered by Indian philosophy, we can draw inspiration from its timeless wisdom and enduring legacy in our quest for knowledge, meaning, and personal fulfilment.

As we face the complex challenges of the 21st century, from climate change to social inequality, Indian philosophy offers us a wealth of ideas, values, and practices that can inspire new ways of thinking and living. By embracing the diverse perspectives and teachings of Indian philosophy, we can cultivate a more holistic, integrated, and compassionate worldview that acknowledges the interconnectedness of all life and the intrinsic value of each individual, community, and ecosystem.

Moreover, Indian philosophy can also catalyse cross-cultural dialogue, collaboration, and understanding. By engaging with Indian thought and learning from its rich traditions, we can foster greater appreciation and respect for our global community's cultural, religious, and intellectual diversity. This spirit of openness, curiosity, and mutual learning can help to break down the barriers of prejudice, ignorance, and misunderstanding that often divide us and pave the way for a more inclusive, just, and peaceful world.

As we continue to explore the relevance of Indian philosophy in today's world, let us remember that the wisdom of the past can offer valuable guidance and inspiration for the present and the future. By integrating the insights and values of Indian philosophy into our personal lives, communities, and global society, we can contribute to creating a more harmonious, sustainable, and fulfilling world for all.

Overview of the Book Series

The structure and focus of the Indian Philosophy Collection

The Indian Philosophy Collection is a comprehensive series of books that delves into the rich and diverse world of Indian philosophical thought. The series is structured in such a way that it provides both a broad overview of the major themes and ideas in Indian philosophy, as well as in-depth explorations of specific schools, thinkers, and texts.

This book, "The Essence of Indian Philosophy: An Overview," serves as the foundation for the entire series, offering a comprehensive introduction to the history, culture, and major themes of Indian philosophy. This first book sets the stage for the subsequent volumes, which provide detailed examinations of specific schools of thought and their key concepts, practices, and texts.

The series' structure allows for a systematic and thorough exploration of Indian philosophy, ensuring readers understand the subject matter deeply. Each book in the series focuses on a specific aspect of Indian philosophy, allowing readers to immerse themselves in the nuances and intricacies of the tradition.

The purpose and intended audience of the series

The purpose of the Indian Philosophy Collection is to make the rich insights and wisdom of Indian philosophical thought accessible to a wide audience, including students, scholars, and general readers interested in exploring non-Western intellectual traditions. The series aims to provide a comprehensive and engaging introduction to Indian philosophy while offering in-depth examinations of specific schools, concepts, and texts for readers who wish to delve deeper into the subject.

The intended audience for the series is diverse. It includes individuals who are new to Indian philosophy and those who have a background in the subject and are seeking a more comprehensive understanding. The series is also suitable for scholars and researchers in philosophy, religious studies, cultural studies, and other disciplines who wish to gain a deeper appreciation of the

Indian intellectual heritage. By presenting the material in a clear, accessible, and engaging manner, the series aims to make the complex ideas and concepts of Indian philosophy comprehensible and appealing to a wide range of readers.

The journey ahead: exploring the depths of Indian philosophy

The Indian Philosophy Collection offers readers a unique opportunity to embark on a fascinating journey through Indian philosophical thought. As the series progresses, readers will be guided through the various schools of thought, from the orthodox systems such as Vedanta, Nyaya, and Yoga to the heterodox traditions like Buddhism, Jainism, and the materialist Charvaka school. Each book in the series will delve into the key concepts, practices, and texts that define these schools, providing readers with a comprehensive understanding of their doctrines and worldviews.

In addition to exploring the various schools of thought, the series will also examine the contributions of influential Indian philosophers and thinkers, such as Adi Shankara, Nagarjuna, Ramanuja, and Abhinavagupta, among others. These figures have shaped the development of Indian philosophy and continue to impact India's intellectual and spiritual landscape and beyond profoundly.

Furthermore, the series will also consider how Indian philosophy has interacted with and been influenced by other intellectual traditions, both within and outside of India. This will include discussions of the impact of foreign invasions and cultural exchanges on the development of Indian thought and the influence of Indian philosophy on Western intellectual traditions.

As readers embark on this journey through the Indian Philosophy Collection, they will be challenged to expand their intellectual horizons, question their assumptions, and develop a more inclusive and pluralistic understanding of reality. By engaging with the diverse ideas, values, and practices that constitute Indian philosophy, readers will better appreciate this rich intellectual tradition and cultivate greater empathy, respect, and understanding for other cultures and worldviews.

Moreover, exploring Indian philosophy in this series can serve as a source of inspiration and wisdom for navigating the challenges of the modern world. As we confront issues such as climate change, social inequality, and cultural conflict, the insights and teachings of Indian philosophy can provide valuable guidance on how to live in harmony with ourselves, others, and the natural world.

In conclusion, the Indian Philosophy Collection offers a unique opportunity for readers to embark on a transformative journey of intellectual and spiritual discovery. By delving into the depths of Indian philosophy, readers will expand their knowledge and understanding of this rich tradition and develop a more compassionate, inclusive, and holistic worldview that can contribute to creating a more just, sustainable, and harmonious world. The journey ahead is enlightening and rewarding as we explore the timeless wisdom and enduring legacy of Indian philosophical thought.

CHAPTER TWO

The Foundational Texts

Introduction to the Foundational Texts

The importance of sacred texts in Indian philosophy

In the rich and diverse world of Indian philosophy, sacred texts play a crucial role in shaping the intellectual, spiritual, and cultural landscape. These texts passed down through generations of scholars and practitioners, serve as repositories of wisdom, insight, and guidance for those who seek to understand and engage with the tradition.

The sacred texts of Indian philosophy are not merely historical artefacts or works of literature; they are living sources of knowledge that continue to inspire and guide individuals on their journey toward self-realisation and spiritual awakening. These texts provide the foundation for the various schools of Indian philosophy and serve as points of reference, debate, and interpretation for generations of thinkers, scholars, and seekers.

The major texts: Vedas, Upanishads, and the Bhagavad Gita

Among the vast corpus of sacred texts in Indian philosophy, three major works are particularly foundational and influential: the

Vedas, the Upanishads, and the Bhagavad Gita. These texts, which span a wide range of philosophical, religious, and cultural themes, have shaped the development of Indian thought and continue to inform the practice and understanding of Indian philosophy today.

The Vedas: The Vedas are the oldest and most revered texts in the Indian philosophical tradition. Composed in Sanskrit, they date back to the second millennium BCE and are considered the foundational scriptures of Hinduism. The Vedas are divided into four main collections: the Rigveda, the Yajurveda, the Samaveda, and the Atharvaveda. Each Veda is further divided into two sections: the Samhitas, which consist of hymns, prayers, and rituals, and the Brahmanas, which provide commentaries and explanations of the rituals.

The Vedas are primarily concerned with religious practices, ceremonies, and the proper performance of rituals. However, they also contain seeds of philosophical thought that would later develop into the complex and sophisticated systems of Indian philosophy. The Vedas emphasise the importance of spiritual and worldly knowledge and the pursuit of truth, righteousness, and self-realisation.

The Upanishads: The Upanishads, also known as Vedanta (meaning "the end of the Vedas"), represent the culmination of Vedic thought. Composed between the 8th and 6th centuries BCE, the Upanishads delve into the deeper spiritual and metaphysical aspects of the Vedic tradition, exploring questions of reality, consciousness, and the ultimate nature of existence.

The Upanishads form the basis of many central concepts in Indian philosophy, such as Brahman (the ultimate reality), Atman (the individual self or soul), and the relationship between the two. They also introduce the notion of moksha, or liberation from the cycle of birth and death, which becomes a central goal for many Indian philosophical systems.

The Upanishads consist of dialogues between sages and their students, often using metaphors, analogies, and stories to convey complex philosophical ideas. These texts have profoundly influenced the development of Hinduism and the various philosophical schools that emerged from the Indian subcontinent.

The Bhagavad Gita: The Bhagavad Gita, often called the "Song of the Lord," is a 700-verse Sanskrit scripture that forms part of the Indian epic, the Mahabharata. Composed around the 2nd century BCE, the Bhagavad Gita is a conversation between Prince Arjuna, a warrior facing a moral dilemma on the battlefield, and Lord Krishna, who serves as his charioteer and spiritual guide.

The Bhagavad Gita synthesises many strands of Indian thought, incorporating ideas from various philosophical schools, including Vedanta, Samkhya, and Yoga. The text addresses many themes, such as the nature of reality, the purpose of human life, the importance of duty and action, and the path to self-realisation.

The Bhagavad Gita has been widely studied and commented upon by generations of scholars and spiritual seekers, and it occupies a central place in the Indian philosophical tradition. Its teachings on balance between action and detachment, the importance of selfless service, and the cultivation of spiritual wisdom have inspired countless individuals throughout history, both within India and beyond.

In summary, the foundational texts of Indian philosophy – the Vedas, Upanishads, and the Bhagavad Gita – provide the bedrock upon which the diverse schools of thought have developed and flourished. These texts offer a wealth of knowledge, insight, and inspiration, addressing fundamental questions about the nature of reality, the purpose of human existence, and the path to self-realisation.

By engaging with these sacred texts, readers can gain a deeper understanding of the intellectual, spiritual, and cultural roots of Indian philosophy and appreciate the rich tapestry of ideas, values, and practices that have shaped the tradition for millennia. As we explore Indian philosophy in the subsequent chapters, we will delve more deeply into the specific schools of thought and thinkers that have been influenced by and built upon the wisdom contained in these foundational texts.

The Vedas: The Ancient Hymns and Rituals

The Rigveda, Yajurveda, Samaveda, and Atharvaveda

The Vedas, the oldest and most revered sacred texts of Indian philosophy, comprise four primary collections: the Rigveda, Yajurveda, Samaveda, and Atharvaveda. These texts represent a different aspect of Vedic knowledge and unique function in ancient India's religious and philosophical life.

Rigveda: The Rigveda is the oldest and most important of the four Vedas, dating to around 1500-1200 BCE. It consists of over 1,000 hymns (suktas) dedicated to various deities, such as Indra, Agni, and Varuna. The hymns primarily focus on invoking the gods for their blessings and protection and expressing gratitude for the natural world and its abundance.

Yajurveda: The Yajurveda is a collection of sacrificial formulas and rituals used to perform Vedic ceremonies. It is divided into two sections: the "white" (Shukla) Yajurveda, which consists mainly of prose, and the "black" (Krishna) Yajurveda, which is a mix of prose and verse. The Yajurveda emphasises the importance of ritualistic actions in maintaining cosmic order and harmony, and it provides detailed instructions for the proper performance of various sacrifices and ceremonies.

Samaveda: The Samaveda is a collection of musical hymns and melodies used in Vedic rituals, particularly the Soma sacrifice. It is primarily derived from the Rigveda and is often considered the "songbook" of the Vedas. The Samaveda emphasises the importance of musical intonation and rhythmic chanting in the performance of sacred ceremonies, highlighting the belief that sound has divine power and can help connect humans with the gods.

Atharvaveda: The Atharvaveda is the most recent of the four Vedas, and it contains a diverse range of hymns, prayers, and incantations that address various practical and everyday concerns, such as health, wealth, and protection from enemies. It also includes philosophical reflections on the nature of reality, the cosmos, and the human condition, as well as spells and charms related to magic and healing.

The significance of the Vedas in shaping Indian thought

The Vedas played a crucial role in shaping ancient India's religious, cultural, and philosophical landscape. As the foundational texts of Hinduism, they provided the basis for developing numerous schools of thought and diverse spiritual practices that emerged over time. The Vedic worldview, which emphasises the importance of cosmic order (rita), moral duty (dharma), and the interdependence between humans and the divine, has greatly influenced the evolution of Indian thought.

Moreover, the Vedas introduced many key concepts that would later be explored and refined by the various philosophical schools of India, such as the concepts of karma (the law of cause and effect), dharma (moral duty), atman (the inner self or soul), and the cyclical nature of time. The Vedas also laid the groundwork for developing Indian metaphysics, epistemology, and ethics, providing a rich and fertile source of inspiration for subsequent generations of thinkers, scholars, and spiritual practitioners.

The philosophical ideas embedded in the hymns and rituals

While the primary focus of the Vedas is on religious rituals and the invocation of deities, these ancient texts also contain philosophical ideas and insights that would later be developed and expanded upon by various Indian philosophical schools. Some of the key philosophical ideas embedded in the Vedas include:

Cosmic order (Rita): The concept of rita, or cosmic order, is central to the Vedic worldview. It signifies the natural and moral order of the universe, which is maintained through the performance of rituals, adherence to moral duties, and the proper functioning of the natural world. This idea reflects a deep appreciation for the interconnectedness of all aspects of existence and the need for harmony between humans, nature, and the divine.

The nature of reality: The Vedas offer glimpses into the ancient Indian understanding of reality and the cosmos. They describe the creation of the universe through the sacrifice of the cosmic being Purusha and the existence of multiple realms or layers of reality, such as the earth, the atmosphere, and the heavens.

The inner self (Atman): The concept of atman, or the inner self, is introduced in the Vedas, though it is more fully developed in the later Upanishads. The atman represents the essence of an individual, the divine spark that resides within each person. The unchanging and eternal aspect of the self transcends the physical body's temporary and perishable nature.

Karma and rebirth: Although the doctrine of karma and the cycle of rebirth are not explicitly detailed in the Vedas, they contain the seeds of these ideas. The Vedas emphasise the importance of actions and their consequences in this life and future lives. The concept of karma, or the law of cause and effect, would later become a central tenet of Indian philosophy, shaping the understanding of morality, duty, and the nature of existence.

The pursuit of knowledge: The Vedas extol the importance of knowledge, wisdom, and the quest for truth. They emphasise the role of the Brahmins, the priestly class, as the custodians of sacred knowledge and the teachers of Vedic wisdom. This emphasis on learning and intellectual inquiry would be carried forward by the various philosophical schools of India, which would continue to explore and debate the nature of reality, consciousness, and the ultimate purpose of human life.

In conclusion, the Vedas represent the foundational texts of Indian philosophy, providing the basis for the diverse schools of thought, religious practices, and cultural traditions that would emerge over the centuries. They offer a rich tapestry of hymns, rituals, and philosophical ideas that have shaped India's religious, moral, and intellectual landscape. As a source of ancient wisdom and insight, the Vedas continue to inspire and inform the study of Indian philosophy, providing a window into the early development of human thought and the quest for understanding the nature of existence, the cosmos, and the human condition.

The Upanishads: The Essence of Vedic Wisdom

The nature and origins of the Upanishads

The Upanishads are a collection of ancient Indian philosophical texts that constitute the final and most profound layer of the Vedic scriptures. They are also known as the Vedanta, which means "the end of the Vedas," signifying both their position within the Vedic corpus and their role in conveying the ultimate wisdom of the Vedas. There are over 200 Upanishads, though only around 10 to 14 are considered principal or authoritative Upanishads, with the rest being classified as minor or later texts.

The Upanishads are believed to have been composed between 800 and 500 BCE, during ancient India's great intellectual and spiritual awakening. They emerged as a response to the increasing ritualism and formalism of the Vedic tradition and as a quest for a deeper understanding of the nature of reality, the self, and the ultimate purpose of human life.

The central themes of the Upanishads

The concepts of Brahman and Atman: One of the most significant contributions of the Upanishads is the introduction and development of the concepts of Brahman and Atman. Brahman represents the ultimate reality or the absolute, the unchanging and eternal essence that pervades and transcends the entire universe. It is the source of all existence, the ground of being, and the ultimate principle underlying all phenomena. The Upanishads describe Brahman as being beyond all attributes and dualities and the essence of all knowledge, consciousness, and bliss.

On the other hand, Atman refers to an individual's true inner self or soul. It is a person's eternal and unchanging essence, transcending the physical body's and ego's temporary and perishable nature. The Upanishads assert that the Atman is identical to Brahman, meaning that the true nature of the self is one with the ultimate reality. This fundamental unity of the individual self and the absolute is expressed in the famous Upanishadic dictum, "Tat Tvam Asi" (That Thou Art).

Pursuing knowledge and self-realisation: The Upanishads emphasise the importance of knowledge, wisdom, and the quest for self-realisation as the ultimate goal of human life. They advocate a process of inquiry, introspection, and meditation to discover the true nature of the self and its unity with Brahman. This pursuit of self-realisation is often described as a journey from ignorance (avidya) to enlightenment (moksha), leading to liberation from the cycle of birth and death and the attainment of eternal bliss and freedom.

The Upanishads present various methods and techniques for self-realisation, such as meditation, yoga, and contemplation of sacred syllables like Om. They also stress the importance of ethical conduct, self-discipline, and detachment from material desires, as prerequisites for spiritual growth and self-discovery.

The influence of the Upanishads on Indian philosophy

The Upanishads have had a profound and lasting impact on Indian philosophy, shaping the development of diverse philosophical schools and religious traditions. Their teachings have influenced Hinduism and other major Indian religions, such as Buddhism and

Jainism, which share many core concepts and values in the Upanishads.

Brahman and Atman's concept and emphasis on self-realisation and spiritual liberation would become central tenets of the Vedanta school of Indian philosophy, based on the interpretation and synthesis of the Upanishadic teachings. Other philosophical schools, such as the Samkhya, Yoga, and Nyaya, also draw upon the insights and ideas of the Upanishads, incorporating their notions of metaphysics, epistemology, and ethics into their respective systems of thought.

The Upanishads have also significantly impacted Indian culture, art, and literature, inspiring countless works of poetry, drama, and music that explore and celebrate the themes of self-discovery, spiritual growth, and the unity of all existence. The Upanishadic wisdom has been transmitted and preserved through generations of scholars, sages, and poets who have contributed to the rich and diverse tradition of Indian philosophical thought.

In addition to their influence within India, the Upanishads have attracted the interest and admiration of thinkers and scholars worldwide. Their universal appeal and timeless insights into the nature of reality, the self, and the ultimate purpose of human life have inspired many Western philosophers, scientists, and writers who have found in the Upanishads a source of wisdom and inspiration for their own intellectual and spiritual quests.

In conclusion, the Upanishads represent a vital and enduring aspect of Indian philosophy, embodying the essence of Vedic wisdom and serving as a foundation for the diverse and complex tapestry of Indian thought. Their teachings on the nature of reality, the self, and the pursuit of self-realisation continue to resonate with seekers of truth and wisdom across time and cultures, offering a profound and timeless vision of the human condition and the ultimate meaning of existence.

The Bhagavad Gita: A Timeless Guide to Life

The context and background of the Bhagavad Gita

The Bhagavad Gita, often called the "Song of the Lord," is a 700-verse Hindu scripture in the Indian epic, the Mahabharata. Set on the battlefield of Kurukshetra, the Gita is a dialogue between Prince Arjuna and the god Krishna, who serves as his charioteer and spiritual guide. Arjuna faces a moral dilemma as he is torn between his duty to fight against his kinsmen and his desire to avoid violence and bloodshed. In response to Arjuna's doubts and questions, Krishna imparts his divine wisdom, offering guidance on the nature of reality, the purpose of human life, and the path to spiritual liberation.

The key concepts of the Bhagavad Gita

Dharma, Karma, and Moksha: One of the central themes of the Bhagavad Gita is the concept of dharma, which refers to the ethical and moral duties an individual must fulfil in accordance with their social and cosmic order. Krishna emphasises the importance of performing one's dharma without attachment to the results to purify the mind and achieve spiritual growth. This notion of selfless action is closely linked to karma, the law of cause and effect that governs the consequences of one's actions. By performing one's duties without attachment, one can transcend the cycle of karma and attain moksha, or liberation from the cycle of birth and death.

The yoga paths to self-realisation: The Bhagavad Gita outlines various paths of yoga or spiritual disciplines that can lead to self-realisation and union with the divine. These paths include:

- **Karma Yoga:** The path of selfless action, in which one performs their duties without attachment to the results, to purify the mind and cultivate inner peace.
- **Bhakti Yoga:** The path of devotion and love, in which one surrender to the divine and seeks to cultivate a personal

relationship with the Supreme Being through acts of worship, prayer, and meditation.

- **Jnana Yoga:** The path of knowledge and wisdom in which one seeks to understand the true nature of reality and the self through study, reflection, and contemplation.
- **Raja Yoga:** The path of meditation and self-discipline, in which one practices various techniques to control the mind, senses, and body, to achieve inner stillness and spiritual insight.

The impact of the Bhagavad Gita on Indian thought and spirituality

The Bhagavad Gita has had a profound and lasting impact on Indian philosophy, religion, and culture. Its teachings have been embraced by various Hindu traditions and followers of other faiths, who have found in the Gita a source of guidance and inspiration for their spiritual journeys. The text has been widely studied, commented upon, and interpreted by numerous scholars, philosophers, and spiritual teachers throughout Indian history. Its influence can be seen in the developing of various schools of thought, including Advaita Vedanta, Vaishnavism, and the Bhakti movement.

The Bhagavad Gita's universal message of dharma, karma, and the paths of yoga has resonated with individuals from diverse backgrounds and cultures, making it one of the world's most beloved and influential spiritual texts. Its emphasis on inner transformation through selfless action, devotion, knowledge, and meditation has inspired countless seekers of truth and wisdom who have found in the Gita a practical and accessible guide to the challenges and dilemmas of human life.

In addition to its spiritual and philosophical significance, the Bhagavad Gita has profoundly impacted Indian art, literature, and popular culture. Its teachings have been expressed in various forms, including poetry, music, dance, and drama, as well as in the visual arts, such as painting and sculpture. The Gita's timeless wisdom has been passed down through generations of artists, writers, and performers, who have sought to convey its message of self-realisation and spiritual liberation in ways that are both engaging and accessible to a wide audience.

In conclusion, the Bhagavad Gita is a foundational text of Indian philosophy, offering a comprehensive and practical guide to the challenges of human existence and the pursuit of spiritual enlightenment. Its teachings on dharma, karma, and the various paths of yoga have shaped the development of Indian thought and spirituality. In contrast, its universal message of self-realisation and inner transformation has resonated with seekers of truth from diverse backgrounds and cultures. As a rich source of wisdom and guidance, the Bhagavad Gita continues to inspire and enlighten individuals on their journey towards a deeper understanding of themselves, their purpose, and their connection to the divine.

The Bhagavad Gita's influence extends beyond India's borders, as its teachings have been embraced by spiritual seekers, philosophers, and scholars worldwide. Its timeless wisdom has been translated into numerous languages, and the Gita has been studied and commented upon by many notable figures, including Mahatma Gandhi, Aldous Huxley, and Ralph Waldo Emerson, to name a few. The universal appeal of the Bhagavad Gita lies in its practical and accessible guidance on overcoming the challenges of human existence and attaining spiritual liberation, making it a valuable resource for individuals seeking to cultivate inner peace, wisdom, and self-realisation in today's complex and rapid changing world.

As we continue to explore the rich and diverse landscape of Indian philosophy, the teachings of the Bhagavad Gita serve as a foundation upon which we can build our understanding of the various schools of thought and their unique contributions to the development of human knowledge and spiritual growth. Through a deeper engagement with the Gita and its timeless message, we can gain valuable insights into the nature of reality, the purpose of human life, and the path to self-realisation and cultivate a greater appreciation for the richness and diversity of Indian philosophical thought.

The Connection between the Foundational Texts

The foundational texts of Indian philosophy – the Vedas, Upanishads, and the Bhagavad Gita – are intricately connected and display a remarkable continuity of ideas and themes. These texts represent the core of Indian thought and have shaped the development of various philosophical schools and spiritual traditions. By examining the connections between these texts, we can gain a deeper understanding of the historical and cultural context in which Indian philosophy evolved and appreciate the richness and diversity of its intellectual heritage.

The development and continuity of ideas across the texts

The Vedas, as the oldest and most revered texts in the Indian tradition, laid the groundwork for the later philosophical developments found in the Upanishads and the Bhagavad Gita. The Vedas consisted of hymns and rituals primarily concerned with worshipping deities and performing sacrificial ceremonies. While these texts may appear predominantly religious, they also contain philosophical ideas that laid the foundation for later developments in Indian thought.

The Upanishads, often regarded as the essence of Vedic wisdom, represent a significant shift in focus from the ritualistic aspects of the Vedas to more abstract and metaphysical concepts. These texts delve deeper into the nature of reality, the self, and the ultimate goal of human existence. The Upanishads introduce the concepts of Brahman (the absolute reality) and Atman (the individual self), which form the basis for many later philosophical and spiritual teachings, including those found in the Bhagavad Gita.

The Bhagavad Gita, as a part of the Indian epic Mahabharata, synthesises the wisdom of the Vedas and the Upanishads into a concise and practical guide to life. The Gita presents a comprehensive philosophical framework that integrates the earlier Vedic ideas and Upanishadic insights with its unique teachings on dharma (duty), karma (action), and moksha (liberation). The Gita's teachings are centred around the concept of yoga, which encompasses various paths to self-realisation and spiritual liberation, such as karma yoga (the path of selfless action), bhakti yoga (the path of devotion), and jnana yoga (the path of knowledge).

The interplay between Vedic rituals, Upanishadic wisdom, and the Gita's teachings

The foundational texts of Indian philosophy are interconnected regarding their historical and cultural context and the development and elaboration of their ideas. The Vedas, emphasising rituals and ceremonies, established a framework for understanding the relationship between the human and the divine and the role of actions in shaping one's destiny. While the Vedas primarily focused on performing rituals to secure material prosperity and spiritual merit, they also contained the seeds of more profound philosophical inquiries that would later be explored in the Upanishads.

The Upanishads represent a significant leap in the evolution of Indian thought as they moved beyond the ritualistic aspects of the Vedas to explore deeper metaphysical questions about the nature of reality, the self, and the ultimate purpose of life. By developing the concepts of Brahman and Atman, the Upanishads sought to uncover the essential unity underlying the apparent diversity of the phenomenal world. They also emphasised the importance of self-realisation and spiritual liberation as the highest goal of human existence, which would later become central themes in the Bhagavad Gita.

The Bhagavad Gita builds upon the ideas of the Vedas and the Upanishads, offering a more accessible and practical guide to living a righteous and fulfilling life. The Gita's teachings on dharma, karma, and moksha reflect a synthesis of the earlier Vedic rituals and the Upanishadic wisdom, offering a coherent and comprehensive framework for understanding the human condition and the path to spiritual liberation. By presenting the concept of yoga, the Gita shows how individuals can integrate the various aspects of their lives – action, devotion, and knowledge – to pursue self-realisation and spiritual growth.

In conclusion, the foundational texts of Indian philosophy – the Vedas, Upanishads, and the Bhagavad Gita – are intricately connected and display a remarkable continuity of ideas and themes. By understanding the connections between these texts, we can appreciate the rich tapestry of Indian thought that has evolved over millennia. The development and interplay of ideas across these texts have shaped India's philosophical and spiritual landscape and continue to inspire seekers of wisdom and spiritual truth worldwide.

The Vedas, Upanishads, and the Bhagavad Gita represent different stages in the evolution of Indian philosophy, each building upon its predecessors' insights while contributing its unique teachings. These texts not only serve as a historical record of the intellectual journey of Indian thinkers but also provide a profound and timeless source of wisdom that continues to be relevant to the modern world.

As we delve deeper into the study of these foundational texts and the various philosophical schools that emerged from them, we will discover the rich diversity of Indian thought and the many ways in which it has contributed to our understanding of the human condition, the nature of reality, and the path to spiritual liberation. By engaging with these texts and their ideas, we will gain a deeper appreciation of India's intellectual and spiritual heritage and, perhaps, find valuable guidance and inspiration for our journey toward wisdom, self-realisation, and inner peace.

The Interpretation and Transmission of the Foundational Texts

The role of oral tradition and written commentaries

The interpretation and transmission of the foundational texts of Indian philosophy were greatly influenced by the oral tradition and the written commentaries that emerged over time. The Vedas, for instance, were primarily transmitted through an oral tradition, with the knowledge passed down from teacher to student over generations. The oral nature of this transmission ensured the preservation and the accurate reproduction of the sacred texts, as the recitation techniques and memorisation methods employed were highly sophisticated and precise.

As Indian philosophical thought evolved, the need for written commentaries to explain and interpret the complex ideas embedded within the foundational texts became apparent. These commentaries, Bhashyas, played a crucial role in elucidating the texts' meaning and significance and fostering intellectual discourse and debate among scholars. The commentaries helped establish the various philosophical schools and systems that emerged from the foundational texts and ensured that the knowledge within them remained accessible and relevant to future generations.

The contributions of key philosophers and commentators

Throughout Indian intellectual history, several key philosophers and commentators have significantly contributed to interpreting and transmitting foundational texts. Among them are:

Adi Shankaracharya (8th century CE) - As the foremost proponent of Advaita Vedanta, Shankaracharya wrote extensive commentaries on the Upanishads, the Brahma Sutras, and the

Bhagavad Gita. His works played a pivotal role in reviving the tradition of non-dualism in Indian philosophy and establishing Advaita Vedanta as a dominant school of thought.

Ramanuja (11th century CE) - Ramanuja was an influential philosopher and theologian who founded the Vishishtadvaita Vedanta school. His commentaries on the Upanishads, the Brahma Sutras, and the Bhagavad Gita emphasised the importance of devotion and the personal relationship with the divine. Ramanuja's works contributed significantly to the development of theistic Vedanta and provided an alternative interpretation of the foundational texts to that of Shankaracharya.

Madhva (13th century CE) - As the founder of the Dvaita Vedanta school, Madhva offered a dualistic interpretation of the foundational texts, emphasising the distinction between the individual soul and the supreme reality. His commentaries on the Upanishads, the Brahma Sutras, and the Bhagavad Gita provided a comprehensive and systematic exposition of the Dvaita philosophy and further enriched the diversity of Indian thought.

Sayana (14th century CE) - Sayana was a renowned Vedic scholar who wrote commentaries on all four Vedas. His work provided valuable insights into the rituals, meaning, and significance of the Vedic hymns, and it remains a vital resource for scholars of Vedic studies today.

Abhinavagupta (10th-11th century CE) - A polymath and an influential figure in Kashmir Shaivism, Abhinavagupta wrote numerous works on various aspects of Indian philosophy, including commentaries on the Upanishads and the Bhagavad Gita. His writings contributed to the understanding and disseminating of the Tantric philosophical tradition and have had a lasting impact on the development of Indian aesthetics and poetics.

The influence of the foundational texts on later Indian philosophical schools

The foundational texts of Indian philosophy served as the bedrock upon which later philosophical schools and systems were built. The Vedas, Upanishads, and the Bhagavad Gita not only laid the groundwork for the orthodox schools of Indian philosophy, such as Nyaya, Vaisheshika, Sankhya, Yoga, Mimamsa, and Vedanta but also inspired the development of heterodox schools like Buddhism and Jainism. These later schools often engaged with the foundational texts in various ways, either by drawing upon their ideas, debating and critiquing them, or offering alternative interpretations and perspectives.

The influence of the foundational texts can also be seen in how they shaped the cultural, social, and religious fabric of Indian society. The Vedas, for instance, provided the basis for the Vedic rituals and ceremonies central to ancient India's religious life. The Upanishads and the Bhagavad Gita, focusing on self-realisation and the pursuit of knowledge, inspired generations of seekers and thinkers to explore the depths of human existence and the nature of reality.

Furthermore, the foundational texts profoundly impacted the development of Indian literature, art, and aesthetics. The Bhagavad Gita, for example, has been a significant source of inspiration for Indian poetry, drama, and narrative traditions. The philosophical ideas embedded in these texts have also influenced the themes and motifs of Indian art and architecture, including depicting the divine and cosmic order and harmony.

In conclusion, the interpretation and transmission of the foundational texts of Indian philosophy have played a crucial role in shaping India's intellectual and cultural landscape. The oral tradition, the written commentaries, and the contributions of key philosophers and commentators have ensured that the knowledge and wisdom contained within these texts remain accessible, relevant, and influential throughout history. The foundational texts have provided the basis for the emergence of diverse philosophical schools and systems and inspired the development of literature, art, and social structures. As a result, the study and understanding of these texts continue to be of utmost importance for anyone seeking to explore the richness and depth of Indian thought and its contributions to the global intellectual heritage.

The Enduring Legacy of the Foundational Texts

The timeless wisdom contained in the Vedas, Upanishads, and the Bhagavad Gita

The foundational texts of Indian philosophy, including the Vedas, Upanishads, and the Bhagavad Gita, have endured for centuries as a testament to the timeless wisdom they contain. These texts offer profound insights into the nature of reality, the human condition, and the ultimate purpose of life. They guide achieving self-realisation, attaining spiritual liberation, and leading a meaningful and fulfilling life.

The Vedas, as the earliest known sacred texts in Indian tradition, encompass a vast range of knowledge, from rituals and hymns to profound philosophical concepts. The Upanishads delve deeper into the metaphysical aspects of existence, exploring the nature of the self, consciousness, and the ultimate reality. The Bhagavad Gita synthesises the wisdom of the Vedas and the Upanishads, providing practical guidance for everyday living through the teachings of Lord Krishna.

The global appeal and influence of these texts

The wisdom in the foundational texts of Indian philosophy has transcended the boundaries of time, geography, and culture. Over the centuries, these texts have attracted the attention and admiration of scholars, philosophers, and spiritual seekers worldwide. Their universal appeal lies in their exploration of fundamental human concerns, such as the quest for meaning, purpose, and fulfilment, as well as their profound insights into the nature of existence, consciousness, and reality.

The influence of these texts can be seen in various intellectual and spiritual traditions across the globe. For instance, the ideas contained in the Upanishads have resonated with Western philosophers such as Schopenhauer, Emerson, and Thoreau, who found inspiration in their exploration of the self and the ultimate reality. The Bhagavad Gita has also been embraced by prominent thinkers and leaders, including Mahatma Gandhi, who saw its teachings as a source of guidance and inspiration for his life and work.

Moreover, the foundational texts have played a crucial role in fostering intercultural dialogue and understanding. By offering insights into India's rich and diverse philosophical heritage, these texts have contributed to a greater appreciation of the common ground shared by different cultural and intellectual traditions.

The continued relevance of the foundational texts in contemporary philosophical discussions and spiritual practice

In today's world, marked by rapid technological advancements and social transformations, the wisdom in the foundational texts of Indian philosophy remains as relevant and valuable as ever. The challenges and complexities of modern life have led to a resurgence of interest in the timeless teachings of these texts as people seek guidance, solace, and a deeper understanding of themselves and the world around them.

The foundational texts offer invaluable insights into the nature of the self and the universe, which can help individuals navigate the challenges of contemporary life. For instance, the concept of dharma, as expounded in the Bhagavad Gita, encourages individuals to fulfil their duties and responsibilities while remaining detached from the fruits of their actions. This teaching can serve as a guiding principle for leading a purposeful and balanced life amidst the pressures and distractions of the modern world.

Additionally, the metaphysical and spiritual insights contained in the Upanishads and the Vedas can contribute to contemporary philosophical debates surrounding consciousness, free will, and the nature of reality. As scientists and philosophers grapple with these questions, the wisdom of these ancient texts can provide valuable perspectives and insights that enrich our understanding of these complex issues.

Furthermore, the spiritual practices and disciplines suggested by the foundational texts, such as meditation, yoga, and self-inquiry, have become increasingly popular in contemporary society. These practices offer a path towards inner peace, self-realisation, and spiritual growth, helping individuals cultivate a sense of wholeness and fulfilment.

In conclusion, the enduring legacy of the foundational texts of Indian philosophy is a testament to the timeless wisdom and profound insights they offer. Their teachings continue to resonate with individuals across the globe, providing guidance, inspiration, and a deeper understanding of the human experience. By engaging with these texts, contemporary philosophers, spiritual seekers, and individuals from all walks of life can enrich their perspectives and find meaningful ways to navigate the complexities of modern life.

As the world becomes increasingly interconnected, the foundational texts of Indian philosophy serve as a bridge between cultures and intellectual traditions, fostering greater intercultural understanding and dialogue. By exploring and appreciating the rich philosophical heritage contained within these texts, we can cultivate a deeper sense of global unity and shared human values.

Ultimately, the Vedas, Upanishads, and the Bhagavad Gita offer a timeless source of wisdom and inspiration that can continue illuminating the path towards personal growth, self-realisation, and spiritual transformation. By engaging with these texts, we can draw upon their insights to enrich our lives, our communities, and our understanding of the world in which we live.

CHAPTER THREE

The Six Orthodox Schools of Indian Philosophy

Introduction to the Orthodox Schools

The classification and defining features of the orthodox schools

The six orthodox schools of Indian philosophy, collectively known as the Shad Darshanas, represent diverse philosophical thought and inquiry rooted in the Vedic tradition. These schools include:

Samkhya: The school of enumerative metaphysics that emphasises the duality of consciousness (Purusha) and material reality (Prakriti).

Yoga: The school focuses on the practical aspects of spiritual discipline and self-realisation through physical and mental practices.

Nyaya: The school of logical analysis and epistemology emphasises acquiring valid knowledge.

Vaisheshika: The school of atomistic metaphysics, which postulates that the universe is composed of indivisible atoms and the qualities that are inhere in them.

Mimamsa (also known as Purva Mimamsa): The school that emphasises the interpretation of Vedic rituals and their practical application in daily life.

Vedanta (also known as Uttara Mimamsa): The school that focuses on the philosophical interpretation of the Upanishads and the nature of ultimate reality.

The orthodox schools are classified as such because they all share a common foundation in the Vedic tradition and accept the authority of the Vedas as divinely revealed knowledge. While each school has its unique approach, emphasis, and methodology, they are all united in their commitment to understanding the ultimate nature of reality and the means to attain spiritual liberation.

The shared foundation in the Vedic tradition

Despite their differences, the six orthodox schools share a common foundation in the Vedic tradition, which serves as the bedrock for their philosophical inquiries. The Vedas, a collection of ancient Indian texts composed in Sanskrit, is considered the oldest and most sacred scriptures in Hinduism. They are believed to have been revealed to the ancient sages or rishis by the divine and passed down through generations via an oral tradition.

Each of the orthodox schools, in its way, seeks to build upon the Vedic teachings and draw from their wisdom to address a wide range of philosophical questions and concerns. The shared foundation in the Vedic tradition provides a common ground for these schools, enabling them to engage in fruitful dialogue and debate while also allowing each school to develop its distinctive insights and perspectives.

For instance, the Samkhya school builds upon the cosmological ideas in the Vedas, refining them into a systematic metaphysical framework that distinguishes between the conscious Purusha and the material Prakriti. Similarly, the Yoga school draws from the spiritual practices and disciplines described in the Vedas, developing a comprehensive system of physical, mental, and ethical practices aimed at self-realisation and spiritual growth.

The Nyaya and Vaisheshika schools, while focusing on logic and metaphysics, respectively, also acknowledge the importance of the Vedic texts as a source of valid knowledge. Both schools seek to establish the veracity of their philosophical claims by grounding them in Vedic authority and developing rigorous methods of inquiry and analysis.

On the other hand, Mimamsa delves deeply into the study and interpretation of the Vedic rituals and their practical applications, emphasising the importance of duty, moral action, and the proper performance of rituals by the Vedic injunctions. Finally, Vedanta, often considered the culmination of Indian philosophical thought, focuses on the philosophical interpretation of the Upanishads, which are considered the essence of Vedic wisdom. Vedanta seeks to understand the nature of ultimate reality, the relationship between the individual and the cosmic Self, and the path to spiritual liberation.

In conclusion, the six orthodox schools of Indian philosophy, while diverse in their approaches and areas of emphasis, are all grounded in the Vedic tradition, which serves as their common source of inspiration and authority. By building upon the rich and varied intellectual heritage of the Vedas, each of these schools has contributed significantly to the development of Indian philosophy and has helped to shape its distinctive character. The shared foundation in the Vedic tradition has not only enabled these schools to engage in meaningful dialogue and debate. Still, it has also provided them with a rich reservoir of spiritual and philosophical insights to draw.

As we delve deeper into each of the six orthodox schools in the following sections, we will come to appreciate the unique contributions that each school has made to Indian philosophical thought, as well as how they have enriched and complemented one another. Exploring these schools will also allow us to reflect on the relevance of their teachings in the contemporary world and consider how their insights might help us navigate the complex challenges of our times.

The orthodox schools of Indian philosophy represent a fascinating and diverse array of perspectives on reality, knowledge, ethics, and spirituality. By studying these schools and engaging with their teachings, we can better understand India's rich intellectual and spiritual heritage and discover new ways of thinking about and approaching the fundamental questions of human existence.

Nyaya: The School of Logical Analysis

Nyaya, often called the School of Logical Analysis, is one of the six orthodox schools of Indian philosophy that has played a crucial role in shaping the country's intellectual landscape. This school is known for its focus on logic, rational inquiry, and epistemology, which has greatly contributed to the development of Indian thought.

The origins and development of Nyaya philosophy

Nyaya philosophy traces its roots back to the ancient sage Gautama, also known as Akṣapāda Gautama, who is credited with the authorship of the foundational text of this school, the Nyaya Sutras. This text dates back to around the 2nd century BCE and lays the groundwork for the logical and epistemological principles that define Nyaya philosophy. Over the centuries, the Nyaya school underwent significant developments and refinements, with notable contributions from philosophers like Vatsyayana, Uddyotakara, and Gangesha Upadhyaya.

The key concepts: Pramanas, categories, and syllogism

Pramanas, or valid means of knowledge, are at the heart of Nyaya philosophy. This school identifies four primary Pramanas: Pratyaksha (perception), Anumana (inference), Upamana (comparison), and Shabda (verbal testimony). These Pramanas serve as the foundation for all knowledge claims and guide the process of rational inquiry.

Another important aspect of Nyaya philosophy is its classification of categories or **Padarthas**. There are 16 categories: substance, quality, action, generality, particularity, and inherence. These categories provide a comprehensive framework for understanding the nature of reality and the relationships between different aspects of existence.

Syllogism, or logical reasoning, is a central component of Nyaya philosophy. Nyaya thinkers developed a formal inference system known as the five-membered syllogism or Panchavayavi. This system consists of five steps: Pratijna (the proposition), Hetu (the reason), Udaharana (the example), Upanaya (the application), and Nigamana (the conclusion). By employing this logical structure, Nyaya philosophers aimed to establish the validity of knowledge claims and engage in rigorous intellectual debates.

The contributions of Nyaya to Indian epistemology and logic

Nyaya's emphasis on logical analysis and epistemology has profoundly impacted the development of Indian thought. Its insistence on rigorous reasoning and using Pramanas to validate knowledge claims helped create a culture of intellectual inquiry and debate, influencing other schools of Indian philosophy.

Nyaya's focus on epistemology led to the development of many important concepts in this field, such as the distinction between direct and indirect knowledge, the theory of error, and the criteria for valid testimony. These contributions have shaped the way Indian philosophers approach the questions of knowledge, truth, and reality.

In the realm of logic, Nyaya's systematic approach to inference and the development of the five-membered syllogism have played a significant role in shaping the Indian logical tradition. Nyaya's logical system provided a foundation for later philosophers to build upon and refine, leading to the development of the Navya-Nyaya (New Nyaya) school in the later medieval period. This school, spearheaded by thinkers like Gangesha Upadadhyaya, further developed the logical and epistemological principles of the Nyaya tradition, making it more sophisticated and precise.

Nyaya's emphasis on logic also led to productive dialogues and debates with other orthodox and heterodox philosophical schools. This interaction resulted in the refinement and clarification of concepts and arguments across various systems of thought, enriching the overall intellectual climate of ancient India.

Furthermore, Nyaya's contributions to logic and epistemology extended beyond philosophy. Its principles found application in fields such as law, linguistics, and hermeneutics, where logical reasoning and the analysis of knowledge claims were of utmost importance.

In conclusion, the Nyaya school of Indian philosophy, focusing on logical analysis and epistemology, has significantly contributed to the development of Indian thought. Its key concepts, such as Pramanas, categories, and syllogism, provided a solid foundation for intellectual inquiry and debate, influencing other philosophical schools and various fields of knowledge. The lasting legacy of Nyaya is a testament to the enduring value of logic and rational inquiry in the pursuit of wisdom and understanding.

Vaisheshika: The School of Particularity and Atomism

The foundation and evolution of Vaisheshika philosophy

The Vaisheshika school of Indian philosophy is often associated with the sage Kanada, believed to have lived around the 6th century BCE. The foundational text of this philosophical system is the Vaisheshika Sutras, attributed to Kanada. Vaisheshika, like Nyaya, is an orthodox school of thought that accepts the authority of the

Vedas. Over time, Vaisheshika developed close ties with Nyaya, and the two schools eventually merged into a single system known as Nyaya-Vaisheshika.

Vaisheshika philosophy underwent several stages of development as it evolved in response to critiques from other schools and incorporated new ideas. Some of the most important later thinkers who contributed to the development of Vaisheshika include Prashastapada, Udayana, and Shankara Mishra.

The key concepts: Padarthas, Dravya, and the atomic theory

The central focus of Vaisheshika is on analysing the fundamental constituents of reality, known as Padarthas. Padarthas are divided into six or seven categories, depending on the thinker: Dravya (substance), Guna (quality), Karma (action), Samanya (generality), Vishesha (particularity), Samavaya (inherence), and, in some later formulations, Abhava (nonexistence). These categories form the building blocks of the Vaisheshika metaphysical system, allowing for a detailed analysis of the world's structure and the relationships between its constituent elements.

Dravya, or substance, is a central concept in Vaisheshika philosophy. There are nine types of substances: earth, water, fire, air, ether, time, space, self (Atman), and mind (Manas). Vaisheshika posits that the first four substances—earth, water, fire, and air—are composed of indivisible, eternal atoms (Anu or Paramanu). These atoms combine in various ways to form complex structures and objects that we perceive in the world. This atomic theory is one of the most distinguishing features of Vaisheshika and sets it apart from other Indian philosophical schools.

The impact of Vaisheshika on Indian metaphysics and natural philosophy

The detailed categorisation of reality in Vaisheshika provided a systematic framework for understanding the world and the relationships between its various components. Its atomic theory, in particular, offered an innovative and sophisticated explanation of the physical world, which influenced later developments in Indian natural philosophy.

Vaisheshika's emphasis on the logical and empirical investigation also had a lasting impact on Indian philosophical thought. Its methodical approach to analysing the nature of reality and its rich ontology made it a valuable resource for subsequent philosophers who sought to understand the world and its underlying principles.

Moreover, the synthesis of Vaisheshika with Nyaya led to the development of a comprehensive system of logic, epistemology, and metaphysics that became one of the dominant philosophical schools in classical India. The shared framework of Nyaya-Vaisheshika allowed for a more robust understanding of knowledge and the world and the development of advanced techniques for logical argumentation and debate.

In addition to its contributions to Indian philosophy, the ideas of the Vaisheshika school also had a broader impact on the intellectual traditions of other cultures. For example, the atomic theory of Vaisheshika was one of the earliest atomistic theories in human history, predating similar ideas in ancient Greece. The school's focus on empirical observation and a systematic classification of reality also resonates with elements of modern scientific inquiry, showcasing the enduring relevance of Vaisheshika's approach to understanding the world.

In summary, the Vaisheshika school has played a significant role in the development of Indian philosophy and natural philosophy. Its unique focus on categorising reality into Padarthas and its atomic theory has left a lasting impression on subsequent generations of thinkers. As an orthodox school closely connected to Nyaya, Vaisheshika contributed to developing a robust and comprehensive philosophical system that has remained influential throughout the history of Indian thought. Furthermore, its emphasis on empirical investigation and systematic analysis of the world resonates with modern scientific approaches, highlighting the enduring relevance and value of the Vaisheshika school in both Indian and global intellectual traditions.

Sankhya: The Dualist School of Thought

The origins and development of Sankhya philosophy

Sankhya, one of the six orthodox schools of Indian philosophy, is a dualist system that dates back to ancient India. The term "Sankhya" means "enumeration" or "number," reflecting the school's systematic and analytical approach to understanding reality. The school's main text, the Sankhya Karika, is attributed to the sage Kapila, traditionally considered the founder of Sankhya philosophy. The Sankhya Karika outlines the basic principles and categories of Sankhya thought, providing a foundation for later commentators and thinkers to expand and refine the system.

Sankhya philosophy has evolved through the works of various philosophers and commentators, including the renowned Ishvarakrishna, believed to have lived around the 4th or 5th century CE. His commentary on the Sankhya Karika, known as the Sankhya Sutras, further developed the Sankhya system and solidified its place as one of the major philosophical schools in India.

The key concepts: Purusha, Prakriti, and the process of evolution

The core concepts of Sankhya philosophy revolve around the dualistic nature of reality, represented by Purusha (consciousness or spirit) and Prakriti (matter or nature). Purusha is considered eternal, unchanging, and devoid of any attributes, while Prakriti is the source of all material existence and possesses the qualities of change and activity.

Purusha: In Sankhya's thought, Purusha represents pure consciousness, the true self, or the unchanging spirit beyond the material world. There are countless Purushas, each existing independently and distinct from others. Purusha is passive, inert, and unaffected by the changes occurring within Prakriti. It is through the interaction between Purusha and Prakriti that the material world is experienced.

Prakriti: Prakriti is the ever-changing material aspect of reality, the source of all material existence, and the driving force behind evolution. Prakriti is composed of three fundamental qualities or Gunas: Sattva(goodness, harmony, and purity), Rajas (passion, energy, and activity), and Tamas (darkness, inertia, and ignorance). These three Gunas interact with one another, resulting in the continuous transformation of Prakriti.

The process of evolution: Sankhya philosophy describes the evolution of the material world as a process originating from the subtlest aspects of Prakriti and gradually manifesting into the gross, tangible reality we experience. The interaction between Purusha and Prakriti triggers the evolution of Prakriti's various components, starting with the subtlest and moving towards the grossest. This evolution unfolds hierarchically, with each successive level emerging from the previous one.

The first product of Prakriti's evolution is Mahat, or cosmic intellect, which represents the universal principle of intelligence. From Mahat, the individual ego (Ahamkara) arises, further differentiated into three categories based on the Gunas. These categories give rise to various subtle and gross elements, as well as the sense organs and motor organs, ultimately resulting in the diverse manifestations of the material world.

The influence of Sankhya on Indian psychology and cosmology

Sankhya philosophy has significantly impacted various aspects of Indian thought, particularly psychology and cosmology. Its detailed analysis of the mind, consciousness, and the material world has provided a framework for understanding the human psyche and the nature of reality. Sankhya's enumeration of the different components of the mind, such as intellect, ego, and the faculties of perception and action, has contributed to a comprehensive understanding of mental processes and the development of Indian psychology.

In addition, Sankhya's cosmology has influenced other Indian philosophical systems, including Yoga, Vedanta, and some aspects of Buddhism. The dualism of Purusha and Prakriti, along with the hierarchical process of evolution, offers a unique perspective on the origin and structure of the universe. The concepts of the three Gunas and their role in creating and transforming the material world have also been integrated into various aspects of Indian thought, including Ayurveda, the traditional Indian system of medicine.

Sankhya philosophy's emphasis on self-realisation and the distinction between the eternal, unchanging Purusha and the ever-changing Prakriti has inspired spiritual seekers and philosophers throughout history. The dualistic worldview of Sankhya has provided a foundation for understanding the human condition and the ultimate goal of liberation from the cycle of birth and death, making it a significant and enduring contribution to Indian philosophy.

Yoga: The Path of Self-Realization

The foundations and growth of Yoga philosophy

Yoga is a comprehensive spiritual practice and philosophy system that originated in ancient India. The term "Yoga" is derived from the Sanskrit root "yuj," which means "to unite" or "to yoke." It refers to the union of the individual consciousness with the universal consciousness or the merging of the individual soul with the supreme reality. Yoga's foundations can be traced back to the pre-Vedic period, with references in the Upanishads and the Bhagavad Gita. The formalisation of Yoga as a systematic path of self-realisation is attributed to the sage Patanjali, who compiled the Yoga Sutras around 400 BCE.

Throughout its history, Yoga has evolved and diversified into various forms and schools, including Hatha Yoga, Raja Yoga, Bhakti Yoga, Karma Yoga, Jnana Yoga, and Tantra Yoga, among others. Each of these forms emphasises different aspects and techniques of spiritual practice. Still, they all share the ultimate goal of self-realisation and liberation from the cycle of birth and death.

The key concepts: the eight limbs of Yoga and the Yoga Sutras of Patanjali

The Yoga Sutras of Patanjali is a foundational text of Yoga philosophy and practice. It is a collection of 196 aphorisms or sutras offering a systematic and structured approach to self-realisation. The Yoga Sutras outline the concept of Ashtanga Yoga, which consists of eight limbs or steps (ashta means eight, and anga means limb) to be followed sequentially. These eight limbs are:

- **Yama:** Ethical principles and moral restraints, which include nonviolence, truthfulness, non-stealing, continence, and non-covetousness.
- **Niyama:** Disciplines and observances, which encompass purity, contentment, austerity, self-study, and surrender to the divine.
- **Asana:** Physical postures that promote stability, flexibility, and the integration of body and mind.
- **Pranayama:** Breath control and regulation help balance the body's energy flow and enhance concentration.
- **Pratyahara:** Withdrawal of the senses from external objects, leading to inner awareness and detachment from the material

world.

- **Dharana:** Concentration or focused attention on a single point or object.
- Dhyana: Meditation or the continuous and uninterrupted flow of consciousness toward the object of concentration.
- **Samadhi:** The state of deep absorption or complete integration, where the individual consciousness merges with the universal consciousness, resulting in self-realisation and liberation.

These eight limbs of Yoga are not meant to be practised in isolation but rather as an integrated and holistic approach to personal transformation and spiritual growth. By following these steps, the practitioner cultivates discipline, self-awareness, and inner peace, ultimately transcending the limitations of the mind and realising the true nature of the self.

The impact of Yoga on Indian spirituality and mind-body practices

The practice of Yoga has had a profound influence on Indian spirituality and the development of various mind-body practices. As a holistic system, Yoga encompasses physical, mental, emotional, and spiritual dimensions of human life, offering a comprehensive approach to well-being and self-realisation. It has inspired numerous spiritual traditions and philosophical schools, including Advaita Vedanta, Kashmir Shaivism, and various forms of Tantra.

Yoga has also significantly shaped the principles and practices of Ayurveda, the ancient Indian system of medicine and healing. Integrating Yoga and Ayurveda offers a holistic approach to health and well-being, emphasising the balance between body, mind, and spirit. This synergy has led to various therapeutic practices, such as Panchakarma, Marma therapy, herbal remedies and dietary guidelines.

In contemporary times, Yoga has transcended its geographical and cultural boundaries, becoming a global phenomenon that appeals to people from diverse backgrounds and belief systems. The physical and mental benefits of yoga, such as increased flexibility, strength, stress reduction, and emotional balance, have been widely recognised and embraced by modern society. This has led to the popularisation of various styles of Yoga, including Ashtanga, Vinyasa, Iyengar, and Bikram Yoga, among others.

Furthermore, the core philosophical teachings of Yoga, such as the concepts of non-attachment, mindfulness, and compassion, have resonated with contemporary spiritual seekers, fostering a deeper understanding of the human experience and the interconnectedness of all beings. This has resulted in integrating Yoga practices and principles into various domains of modern life, including education, healthcare, and the corporate world.

In conclusion, the philosophy and practice of Yoga have had a profound and lasting impact on Indian spirituality and mind-body practices. Its holistic approach to personal transformation and self-realisation has inspired countless seekers throughout history and continues influencing contemporary thought and culture. As a timeless and universal path, Yoga offers valuable insights and tools for navigating the challenges of modern life, fostering inner peace, and cultivating a deeper connection with the self and the world around us.

Mimamsa: The School of Ritual and Exegesis

The origins and development of Mimamsa philosophy

Mimamsa, also known as Purva Mimamsa (the earlier inquiry), is one of the six orthodox schools of Indian philosophy. It primarily focuses on interpreting Vedic texts, specifically the Brahmanas and the Samhitas, concerned with ritual and sacrificial practices. The school traces its origins to the ancient sage Jaimini, who composed the foundational text, the Mimamsa Sutras, around the 5th century

BCE.

Mimamsa philosophy developed in response to the need for a systematic method to understand and apply the complex rituals prescribed in the Vedic texts. Over time, this school produced many commentaries and exegetical works by several prominent philosophers, including Sabara, Kumarila Bhatta, and Prabhakara. These scholars contributed to elaborating and refining Mimamsa principles, establishing it as a distinct and influential school of thought within Indian philosophy.

The key concepts: Dharma, interpretation, and Vedic injunctions

Dharma: Central to Mimamsa philosophy is the concept of Dharma, which can be loosely translated as duty or righteousness. Mimamsa holds that the performance of Vedic rituals and the adherence to moral and ethical injunctions are essential for maintaining cosmic order and ensuring individual well-being. According to Mimamsa, Dharma derives from the correct interpretation and application of Vedic injunctions, which prescribe specific rituals and duties for individuals based on their social and personal contexts.

Interpretation: Mimamsa scholars developed a sophisticated hermeneutical system to interpret and understand the meaning of the Vedic texts. They applied various principles of linguistic analysis, such as context, grammar, and etymology, to decipher the intention of the Vedic seers and determine the correct performance of rituals. The Mimamsa school's rigorous approach to textual interpretation laid the foundation for the development of Indian hermeneutics and contributed significantly to the study of Sanskrit grammar and linguistics.

Vedic injunctions: Mimamsa emphasises the authority of the Vedas and the performance of Vedic rituals. According to Mimamsa, the purpose of the Vedas is to instruct individuals in performing sacrificial rituals necessary to attain specific worldly and spiritual goals. The Mimamsa school recognises various categories of Vedic injunctions, such as Vidhi (prescriptive), Nishedha (prohibitive), and Arthavada (explanatory). These injunctions provide detailed guidance on the performance of rituals, the selection of offerings, and the proper recitation of mantras, among other aspects.

The contributions of Mimamsa to Indian hermeneutics and ritual theory

Hermeneutics: Mimamsa's rigorous approach to Vedic interpretation has profoundly impacted the field of Indian hermeneutics. The principles and methods developed by Mimamsa scholars have been widely adopted and adapted by other philosophical schools to interpret their foundational texts. The attention to detail, context, and linguistic nuances in Mimamsa exegesis has enriched the understanding and appreciation of the Vedas and other classical Indian texts.

Ritual theory: Mimamsa's focus on the performance of Vedic rituals and its insistence on the importance of the correct interpretation of the Vedic texts has contributed significantly to the development of Indian ritual theory. The school's elaborate explanations of the significance, symbolism, and structure of rituals have provided a systematic framework for understanding the role of rituals in Indian religious and social life. Mimamsa's emphasis on the practical aspects of ritual performance has also influenced how rituals are conducted in various Indian traditions, ensuring that they adhere to the prescribed norms and guidelines.

Influence on other philosophical schools: The insights and methods developed by Mimamsa scholars have been adopted and adapted by other Indian philosophical schools, particularly in epistemology, logic, and hermeneutics. For instance, the Nyaya school borrowed Mimamsa's theory of knowledge (Pramanas) to develop its epistemological system. In contrast, the Vedanta school utilised Mimamsa's principles of textual interpretation to understand and expound upon the Upanishads.

In conclusion, the Mimamsa school of Indian philosophy has significantly contributed to the development of Indian thought, particularly in hermeneutics, ritual theory, and the interpretation of sacred texts. By emphasising the importance of the correct understanding and performance of Vedic rituals, Mimamsa has played a crucial role in shaping Indian religious and social life. Its rigorous approach to textual analysis and its emphasis on the authority of the Vedas have influenced various other Indian philosophical schools, ensuring that the Mimamsa tradition remains an integral part of the broader Indian intellectual landscape.

Vedanta: The School of Ultimate Reality

The foundations and evolution of Vedanta philosophy

Vedanta, which means "the end of the Vedas," is a school of Indian philosophy that focuses on the teachings of the Upanishads, the Bhagavad Gita, and the Brahma Sutras. These texts are considered the culmination of Vedic wisdom and contain profound insights into the nature of reality, self, and consciousness. The origins of Vedanta can be traced back to the ancient Indian sages who composed the Upanishads, with further development occurring over many centuries through the commentaries and interpretations of various philosophers and scholars.

The Brahma Sutras, attributed to the sage Badarayana or Vyasa, is a central text in Vedanta, which systematises the teachings of the Upanishads into a coherent philosophical framework. Throughout its history, Vedanta has witnessed the emergence of various sub-schools and interpretations, each offering unique perspectives on the nature of reality and the path to self-realisation.

The key concepts: Brahman, Atman, and the three primary Vedantic schools

Brahman: Vedanta posits the existence of an ultimate reality, Brahman, which is the absolute, infinite, eternal, and unchanging principle that underlies the entire cosmos. Brahman is considered the source of all creation, the essence of everything that exists, and the ultimate goal of human spiritual pursuit. In Vedanta, the realisation of the identity of one's self with Brahman is the key to attaining liberation from the cycle of birth and death.

Atman: Atman is the individual self or soul, often described as a reflection or a spark of Brahman within each person. According to Vedanta, the ultimate goal of human life is to realise the unity of Atman with Brahman, thereby achieving self-realisation and liberation.

The three primary Vedantic schools: Over time, various interpretations of Vedanta have emerged, leading to the development of three main sub-schools: Advaita Vedanta, Vishishtadvaita Vedanta, and Dvaita Vedanta.

- **Advaita Vedanta:** Advaita, meaning "non-dual," is the most prominent and influential Vedanta sub-school. Founded by the philosopher Adi Shankara, Advaita Vedanta posits that the individual self (Atman) is identical to the ultimate reality (Brahman). It asserts that any perceived distinctions between Atman and Brahman are illusory, and the ultimate goal of human life is to transcend this illusion through self-realisation. According to Advaita, the world we experience is merely an illusion (Maya), and only Brahman exists as the sole, non-dual reality.

- **Vishishtadvaita Vedanta:** Vishishtadvaita, meaning "qualified non-dualism," was founded by the philosopher Ramanuja. This sub-school asserts that while Atman and Brahman are identical, the individual self remains distinct from the ultimate reality. The relationship between the individual self and Brahman is like that of a part of the whole. Vishishtadvaita emphasises the importance of devotion (Bhakti) to a personal God (usually Vishnu) to attain self-realisation and liberation.

- **Dvaita Vedanta:** Dvaita, meaning "dualism," was founded by the philosopher Madhva. This sub-school posits that there is a fundamental distinction between the individual self (Atman) and the ultimate reality (Brahman). According to Dvaita, Brahman is an entirely separate, supreme being, and the individual self can never become one with it. In Dvaita Vedanta, human life's ultimate goal is to develop a deep, loving relationship with the supreme being through devotion (Bhakti) and worship.

The influence of Vedanta on Indian metaphysics and spiritual thought

Throughout its history, Vedanta has profoundly impacted Indian thought, spirituality, and culture. Its teachings have inspired various religious and spiritual traditions, including Hinduism, Buddhism, and Jainism. Many of the core tenets of Vedanta, such as the unity of Atman and Brahman, the concept of Maya, and the pursuit of self-realisation, have become central themes in Indian spiritual practice and have also influenced the development of Indian art, literature, and science.

In contemporary times, Vedanta continues to be a significant force in shaping India's spiritual and philosophical landscape and beyond. Its timeless wisdom has gained global recognition, with many seekers from around the world exploring its profound insights into the nature of reality, self, and consciousness. As a result, Vedanta has become a key component of intercultural understanding and dialogue, fostering an appreciation of the rich philosophical heritage of India and its potential to address modern challenges and promote personal and collective well-being.

The Interconnectedness of the Orthodox Schools

The common ground and points of divergence among the schools

The six orthodox schools of Indian philosophy, despite their distinctive features and focus areas, share a common ground in their adherence to the Vedic tradition. They all accept the authority of the Vedas and, to varying degrees, draw upon the foundational texts of Indian philosophy, such as the Upanishads and the Bhagavad Gita. These schools also share a general orientation towards pursuing knowledge and self-realisation, emphasising understanding the nature of reality, the self, and the ultimate purpose of human existence.

However, the orthodox schools also exhibit significant points of divergence in their metaphysical, epistemological, and ethical views. For instance, while Sankhya posits a dualist metaphysics that distinguishes between the eternal consciousness (Purusha) and the material world (Prakriti), Advaita Vedanta asserts the ultimate non-duality of Brahman and Atman, emphasising that the phenomenal world is an illusory manifestation of the ultimate reality. Similarly, the epistemological frameworks of the schools differ, with Nyaya focusing on a systematic approach to logic and reasoning. At the same time, Mimamsa emphasises the interpretation of Vedic texts and rituals as the primary means of acquiring knowledge. The ethical perspectives of these schools also vary, with Yoga outlining a path of self-realisation through spiritual and physical practices. At the same time, Vedanta discusses the ultimate goal of liberation (moksha) through the realisation of the unity of the self and the ultimate reality.

The philosophical debates and cross-pollination of ideas

Throughout the history of Indian philosophy, the orthodox schools have engaged in philosophical debates and exchanges that have enriched their respective intellectual traditions. These debates allowed each school to refine and strengthen its arguments and address the criticisms and challenges posed by rival schools. Such interactions have led to a cross-pollination of ideas, with various schools incorporating and adapting elements from one another.

For example, the development of the logic and epistemology of Nyaya influenced the epistemological discussions in other schools, such as Vedanta and Mimamsa, leading to the refinement of their respective methods of inquiry and argumentation. Similarly, the metaphysical concepts of Sankhya, such as the distinction between Purusha and Prakriti, have informed the discussions of the nature of reality in other schools, including Yoga and Vedanta. Incorporating Yoga's practical techniques into the spiritual practices of other schools, such as Vedanta, is another example of the cross-pollination of ideas among the orthodox schools.

The holistic approach to understanding Indian philosophy

To gain a comprehensive understanding of Indian philosophy, it is essential to recognise the interconnectedness of the orthodox schools and to approach their teachings as part of a larger philosophical framework. Each school offers unique insights and perspectives that, when considered collectively, provide a multifaceted and holistic understanding of the complex philosophical landscape of ancient India.

Furthermore, the synthesis of ideas from different schools has often led to the development of new philosophical systems and approaches that transcend the boundaries of the original traditions. For instance, integrating Sankhya's metaphysics with Yoga's practical techniques has given rise to a rich and diverse range of spiritual practices catering to various temperaments and inclinations. Similarly, blending Nyaya's logical analysis with

Vedanta's non-dualist metaphysics has produced sophisticated systems of thought that combine rigorous reasoning with profound spiritual insights.

In conclusion, the interconnectedness of the orthodox schools of Indian philosophy is a testament to the richness and diversity of India's intellectual heritage. By appreciating the common ground and the points of divergence among these schools and recognising the cross-pollination of ideas that have taken place throughout their history, one can gain a deeper and more nuanced understanding of the vast and intricate tapestry of Indian thought and its enduring legacy. This holistic approach enables us to appreciate the richness of each school's contributions to the overall philosophical discourse and the development of Indian intellectual and spiritual traditions.

Moreover, the study of the interconnectedness of the orthodox schools allows us to recognise the complex dynamics that have shaped the evolution of Indian philosophy over time. By examining the various interactions, debates, and exchanges among these schools, we can trace the historical development of ideas and how they have been adapted, refined, and reinterpreted in response to new challenges and contexts.

The contemporary relevance of this holistic approach to Indian philosophy lies in its potential to foster a more inclusive and integrative understanding of the diverse philosophical traditions of the world. By recognising the common ground and shared aspirations that underlie the various schools of Indian philosophy, we can cultivate a spirit of openness and dialogue that encourages mutual learning and respect among different intellectual and spiritual traditions.

In a world marked by increasing cultural and religious tensions, studying the interconnectedness of the orthodox schools of Indian philosophy can serve as a powerful reminder of the potential for unity and harmony within diversity. By engaging with the rich and multifaceted landscape of Indian thought, we can draw inspiration and guidance for addressing the complex challenges of our contemporary world and contribute to the ongoing quest for truth, wisdom, and self-realisation that lies at the heart of all human endeavours.

Furthermore, the holistic approach to understanding Indian philosophy offers valuable insights for addressing contemporary issues in various fields, such as psychology, ethics, and environmental studies. For example, the psychological insights provided by the Sankhya and Yoga schools can contribute to a deeper understanding of human consciousness and mental well-being. In contrast, the ethical discussions in the Vedanta and Mimamsa schools can inform our approach to morality and social justice questions.

In environmental studies, the Vaisheshika school's atomic theory and the metaphysical concepts of interconnectedness found in the Vedanta school can offer alternative perspectives on the nature of matter and the interdependence of all living beings. These perspectives can inspire new ways of thinking about our relationship with the natural world and the importance of ecological sustainability.

By embracing a holistic approach to studying Indian philosophy, we can draw upon the rich resources of India's intellectual heritage to deepen our understanding of the human condition and explore new pathways for personal and collective growth. By studying the interconnectedness of the orthodox schools, we can also foster a spirit of intercultural understanding and dialogue that promotes global harmony and the realisation of our shared humanity.

In summary, the interconnectedness of the orthodox schools of Indian philosophy underscores the importance of a holistic approach to understanding Indian thought and its enduring legacy. By appreciating the common ground, points of divergence, and cross-pollination of ideas among these schools, we can gain a more comprehensive and nuanced understanding of the rich and diverse landscape of Indian philosophy. This approach deepens our appreciation of India's intellectual and spiritual traditions. It offers valuable insights and perspectives that can contribute to addressing contemporary challenges in various fields, fostering intercultural understanding and dialogue, and promoting global harmony and the realisation of our shared humanity.

The Lasting Impact of the Orthodox Schools

The enduring legacy of the six schools in Indian philosophical thought

The six orthodox schools of Indian philosophy have left an indelible mark on India's intellectual and spiritual landscape. Over the centuries, these schools have collectively contributed to developing a rich and complex tapestry of thought, spanning diverse topics such as metaphysics, epistemology, ethics, logic, and cosmology. The foundational concepts, ideas, and practices of these schools continue to shape the way Indian philosophy is understood and approached, both within India and around the world.

The influence of the orthodox schools on later Indian intellectual traditions

The orthodox schools have not only shaped the course of Indian philosophical thought but have also influenced various other intellectual traditions in India. For instance, the Sankhya school's dualism and its concepts of Purusha and Prakriti have profoundly impacted the development of Indian psychology and medicine, particularly in the Ayurvedic tradition. Similarly, the emphasis on logic and systematic inquiry in the Nyaya and Vaisheshika schools has influenced Indian mathematics, astronomy, and other scientific disciplines. The ethical and spiritual teachings of the Yoga and Vedanta schools have inspired countless thinkers, poets, and mystics, giving rise to a rich tradition of devotional literature and contemplative practices.

The orthodox schools have also played a crucial role in shaping the later Indian philosophical schools, including the various sub-schools of Vedanta, such as Advaita, Vishishtadvaita, and Dvaita, as well as the diverse movements within the Bhakti tradition. The intellectual debates and cross-pollination of ideas between the orthodox schools and the heterodox traditions, like Buddhism and Jainism, have further enriched the Indian philosophical heritage and contributed to developing a unique and dynamic intellectual culture.

The continued relevance of the orthodox schools in contemporary philosophical discussions and spiritual practice

In today's world, the ideas and insights of the orthodox schools remain relevant, offering timeless wisdom that can be applied to various aspects of modern life. For instance, the Yoga school's emphasis on physical and mental well-being has become more relevant than ever in the face of increasing stress and lifestyle-related health issues. Yoga has gained global recognition for its holistic approach to health and well-being, transcending cultural and geographical boundaries.

Furthermore, the focus on logical reasoning and epistemology in the Nyaya school can provide valuable insights into contemporary debates on knowledge and truth. Similarly, the metaphysical concepts of the Sankhya and Vedanta schools can offer fresh perspectives on understanding the nature of reality, consciousness, and the self, sparking new conversations in the fields of philosophy, psychology, and neuroscience.

The ethical teachings of these schools can also inform modern discussions on morality, social justice, and environmental stewardship. For example, the concept of Dharma in the Mimamsa school, which emphasises the importance of righteous action and adherence to moral principles, can inspire contemporary ethical frameworks that promote harmony, justice, and sustainability.

Lastly, the enduring appeal of orthodox schools lies in their ability to foster intercultural understanding and dialogue. As people from diverse backgrounds and belief systems engage with these schools' rich and varied ideas, they can discover shared values and aspirations, promoting greater tolerance, empathy, and mutual respect. In this way, the lasting impact of the six orthodox schools of Indian philosophy extends far beyond academic inquiry and spiritual practice, contributing to creating a more inclusive, compassionate, and enlightened global society.

Conclusion

In conclusion, the six orthodox schools of Indian philosophy showcase the remarkable diversity and richness of the Indian intellectual tradition. Each school offers a unique perspective on reality, knowledge, ethics, and spirituality, reflecting the multifaceted nature of human experience and the quest for truth. Collectively, they provide a comprehensive understanding of the philosophical underpinnings of Indian thought, embodying the spirit of inquiry, introspection, and synthesis that has characterised Indian philosophy throughout its history.

Exploring the six orthodox schools is essential for anyone seeking a deeper understanding of Indian thought. Delving into each school's foundational texts, concepts, and ideas, one can gain valuable insights into the key themes and concerns that have shaped Indian philosophical discourse. Studying orthodox schools offers a unique opportunity to appreciate the interplay between various philosophical systems as they engage in dialogue, debate, and mutual enrichment.

The continued relevance of the orthodox schools in contemporary philosophical discussions and spiritual practice is evident in the resurgence of interest in Indian thought worldwide. Their insights into the nature of reality, self, consciousness, ethics, and spiritual practice offer valuable guidance for addressing modern existential challenges and ethical dilemmas. The emphasis on inner transformation, self-realisation, and cultivating wisdom and compassion in these schools can inspire individuals to lead more fulfilling, purposeful, and ethically grounded lives.

Studying the six orthodox schools of Indian philosophy enriches our understanding of the human condition and the enduring quest for meaning, purpose, and transcendence. By engaging with these schools and their rich intellectual heritage, we can draw inspiration from the wisdom of the past while also gaining fresh insights and perspectives that can inform and enrich our lives in the present.

Our collective responsibility is to preserve, study, and share the rich intellectual heritage of the six orthodox schools of Indian philosophy, ensuring that their insights and wisdom continue to inform and inspire future generations. By embracing the spirit of inquiry, introspection, and synthesis characterising these schools, we can contribute to a more inclusive and enlightened global discourse, fostering greater tolerance, understanding, and respect for diverse perspectives.

As we continue to confront the challenges of the 21st century, the six orthodox schools of Indian philosophy offer a unique and invaluable resource for cultivating resilience, adaptability, and wisdom in the face of adversity. By drawing on the insights and teachings of these ancient traditions, we can develop the intellectual tools and moral compass needed to navigate the complex and uncertain terrain of our rapidly changing world, forging new pathways towards a more just, sustainable, and flourishing global society.

The six orthodox schools of Indian philosophy offer a unique window into the richness and diversity of Indian thought, providing an invaluable resource for individuals and societies seeking to navigate the complexities of the contemporary world. Engaging with these schools and their teachings can help us better understand the human experience, cultivate inner wisdom and spiritual growth, and contribute to the ongoing dialogue between diverse cultures and intellectual traditions.

Ultimately, the study and appreciation of the six orthodox schools of Indian philosophy serve as a testament to philosophical inquiry's enduring power and relevance in the quest for meaning, purpose, and transcendence. By exploring and engaging with these schools, we can not only enrich our understanding of the world and our place within it but also contribute to the ongoing evolution of human thought, ensuring that the wisdom of the past continues to illuminate and guide our path towards a more enlightened, compassionate, and harmonious future.

CHAPTER FOUR

The Heterodox Schools of Indian Philosophy

Introduction to the Heterodox Schools

The classification and defining features of the heterodox schools

In addition to the six orthodox schools of Indian philosophy, several heterodox schools have significantly contributed to the rich tapestry of Indian thought. The heterodox schools are classified as such primarily because they do not accept the authority of the Vedas, which distinguishes them from the orthodox schools. These schools often offer alternative perspectives on various aspects of reality, knowledge, and ethics, and their views have had a lasting impact on Indian philosophical discourse.

The main heterodox schools include Jainism, Buddhism, and the materialist school of Charvaka. Each school has developed unique philosophical systems and approaches, often in response to or dialogue with the orthodox schools.

Jainism: Founded by Mahavira, the 24th Tirthankara, Jainism offers a pluralistic and non-absolutist approach to reality, emphasising the importance of non-violence (ahimsa) spiritual purification through self-discipline and asceticism.

Buddhism: Established by Siddhartha Gautama, known as the Buddha, Buddhism is centred around the Four Noble Truths and the Eightfold Path, offering a practical and compassionate path to enlightenment through mindfulness, meditation, and ethical conduct.

Charvaka: Also known as the Lokayata school, Charvaka is a materialist and hedonistic philosophical system that denies the existence of an afterlife, karma, and any divine authority. It emphasises the importance of sensory experience, logical reasoning, and the pursuit of pleasure as the ultimate goal in life.

The distinctive approaches to philosophical inquiry

While the heterodox schools of Indian philosophy differ in their core beliefs and practices, they are committed to independent inquiry, critical analysis, and rational argumentation. Unlike the orthodox schools, which base their philosophical systems on the authority of the Vedas, the heterodox schools often reject scriptural authority in favour of empirical evidence, logical reasoning, and personal experience. This emphasis on free inquiry and intellectual autonomy has contributed to developing diverse and innovative philosophical perspectives within the heterodox tradition.

Jainism: Jain philosophy is characterised by its emphasis on anekantavada, the doctrine of manifold aspects, which asserts that reality is multifaceted and cannot be captured by any single viewpoint or dogma. This pluralistic approach encourages intellectual humility, tolerance, and open-mindedness, fostering dialogue and debate among Jain thinkers and between Jainism and other philosophical schools. In addition, Jainism's focus on non-violence (ahimsa) and the interconnectedness of all living beings has led to the development of a robust ethical system that emphasises compassion, restraint, and environmental responsibility.

Buddhism: Buddhist philosophy is marked by its emphasis on the impermanence (anicca), suffering (dukkha), and non-self (anatta) of all phenomena. These insights form the foundation of the Four Noble Truths, which outline the nature of suffering, its cause, its cessation, and the path to liberation. Buddhist philosophical inquiry is characterised by its pragmatic and experiential orientation, focusing on meditation and mindfulness practices to cultivate wisdom, compassion, and inner peace. This practical approach has given rise to various philosophical schools within Buddhism, including the Theravada, Mahayana, and Vajrayana traditions, each with distinctive doctrines, practices, and texts.

Charvaka: The Charvaka school of Indian philosophy is notable for its materialist and empiricist approach to knowledge and reality. Charvaka philosophers argue that sensory perception is the only reliable source of knowledge, and they reject the existence of any supernatural entities or transcendent realities beyond the material world. This sceptical stance has led Charvaka thinkers to challenge many of the core assumptions and beliefs of the orthodox schools, such as the doctrines of karma, reincarnation, and the authority of the Vedas. Furthermore, Charvaka's hedonistic ethics, which emphasise the pursuit of pleasure and the avoidance of pain as the highest good, starkly contrast the ascetic and other-worldly values espoused by many other Indian philosophical schools.

The heterodox schools of Indian philosophy have played a crucial role in shaping the intellectual landscape of India and have contributed significantly to the development of diverse and innovative philosophical perspectives. By challenging conventional wisdom and promoting critical inquiry, these schools have enriched and expanded the scope of Indian philosophical thought, fostering a vibrant and dynamic tradition of intellectual debate and exchange.

Their distinctive approaches to philosophical inquiry, marked by a commitment to empirical evidence, logical reasoning, and experiential knowledge, have laid the groundwork for a rich and varied tapestry of ideas, concepts, and practices that continue to inform and inspire contemporary philosophical discussions and spiritual practice.

In conclusion, the heterodox schools of Indian philosophy offer valuable insights and perspectives that complement and enrich the teachings of the orthodox schools. By exploring the distinctive approaches to reality, knowledge, and ethics found in Jainism, Buddhism, and Charvaka, we can gain a deeper understanding of the diversity and richness of Indian thought and appreciate the unique contributions of these schools to the ongoing evolution of human thought and experience. As we continue to engage with the ideas and insights of the heterodox schools, we can draw on their intellectual and spiritual resources to address the challenges and opportunities of the modern world, fostering a more inclusive, tolerant, and interconnected global community that values the richness and complexity of the human experience.

Furthermore, the heterodox schools of Indian philosophy remind us of the importance of embracing intellectual curiosity, open-mindedness, and a spirit of inquiry in our quest for truth, wisdom, and understanding. By engaging with these schools' diverse perspectives and approaches, we can cultivate the intellectual humility and flexibility needed to navigate the complexities of the contemporary world, forging new pathways towards a more just, compassionate, and enlightened future.

Ultimately, the study and appreciation of the heterodox schools of Indian philosophy are not merely an intellectual exercise or historical curiosity but a vital and transformative journey into the depths of human experience, the mysteries of existence, and the limitless potential of the human spirit. By embracing and integrating the wisdom of these schools into our lives, we can cultivate the inner resources, ethical values, and spiritual vision needed to create a more enlightened, compassionate, and interconnected world that honours the dignity, worth, and potential of every living being.

Buddhism: The Middle Way and the Four Noble Truths

Buddhism, one of the most influential heterodox schools of Indian philosophy, traces its roots to the life and teachings of Siddhartha Gautama, who came to be known as the Buddha or "the enlightened one." Born into a life of privilege and luxury, Siddhartha embarked on a spiritual quest to understand the nature of human suffering and discover a path to transcend it. Through deep meditation and contemplation, he achieved enlightenment and began sharing his insights with others, thus laying the foundation for the Buddhist tradition.

The Four Noble Truths are at the core of Buddhism, which serve as a framework for understanding the nature of suffering and the path to liberation. The First Noble Truth, the truth of suffering (Dukkha), posits that life is inherently characterised by impermanence, dissatisfaction, and suffering. The Second Noble Truth, the truth of the origin of suffering (Samudaya), attributes the root cause of suffering to craving and attachment. The Third Noble Truth, the truth of the cessation of suffering (Nirodha), offers hope by asserting that it is possible to overcome suffering and achieve a state of inner peace and liberation known as Nirvana. Finally, the Fourth Noble Truth, the truth of the path leading to the cessation of suffering (Magga), outlines the practical steps one must take to attain Nirvana, which is encapsulated in the Eightfold Path. This path consists of the right understanding, right intention, right speech, right action, right livelihood, right effort, right mindfulness, and right concentration. By following these principles, individuals can break free from the cycle of suffering and attain spiritual liberation.

Over time, Buddhism evolved into three main traditions: Theravada, Mahayana, and Vajrayana. Theravada, the oldest of the three, is primarily practised in Southeast Asia and emphasises personal enlightenment through meditation and strict adherence to the Buddha's original teachings. Mahayana, the largest and most widespread tradition, developed in India and later spread to East Asia, including China, Korea, and Japan. Mahayana emphasises the ideal of the Bodhisattva, a compassionate being who seeks to attain enlightenment for themselves and help all sentient beings achieve liberation. Vajrayana, also known as Tantric or Esoteric Buddhism, primarily found in Tibet and parts of the Himalayas, incorporate esoteric rituals, mantras, and visualisations to accelerate enlightenment.

Buddhism has profoundly impacted Indian philosophical thought and has spread its teachings and practices across the globe. As a heterodox school, it challenged the authority of the Vedic tradition and introduced new perspectives on the nature of reality, consciousness, and the path to spiritual liberation. By emphasising the importance of personal experience, introspection, and compassion, Buddhism provided an alternative approach to understanding the human condition and offered practical guidance for alleviating suffering.

The global spread of Buddhism has been facilitated by the appeal of its universal teachings and its adaptability to different cultural contexts. Throughout history, Buddhist ideas and practices have been integrated into various societies, enriching local customs and beliefs and transforming the Buddhist tradition. This cross-cultural exchange has resulted in diverse Buddhist schools, practices, and artistic expressions that continue to flourish in both traditional and contemporary settings.

In today's world, the teachings of Buddhism remain relevant and continue to inspire millions of people across the globe. As a philosophical system, it offers insights into the nature of suffering, the human mind, and the potential for inner transformation. Moreover, the ethical principles of Buddhism, such as nonviolence, compassion, and interdependence, resonate with contemporary concerns about social justice, environmental sustainability, and global harmony.

In conclusion, Buddhism's profound impact on Indian thought and its global reach underscore the enduring significance of this heterodox school of philosophy. By exploring the teachings of the Buddha and the rich tapestry of Buddhist traditions, one can gain a deeper understanding of the human experience and cultivate the wisdom and compassion necessary to navigate the challenges of modern life. Furthermore, studying Buddhism offers valuable insights into the development of Indian philosophical thought and highlights the importance of considering alternative perspectives and approaches to understanding reality.

The story of Buddhism, as well as the other heterodox schools of Indian philosophy, demonstrates the rich diversity and intellectual vibrancy that characterised the ancient Indian philosophical landscape. By engaging with these traditions, one can not only appreciate the depth and breadth of Indian thought but also uncover timeless wisdom that can inform and enrich our contemporary understanding of the world and our place within it.

The heterodox schools of Indian philosophy, including Buddhism, are a testament to the power of human inquiry and the enduring quest for knowledge, truth, and spiritual fulfilment. By exploring these diverse systems of thought, we can deepen our appreciation for India's cultural and intellectual heritage and contribute to a more nuanced and inclusive understanding of the global philosophical tradition.

Jainism: The Path of Nonviolence and Spiritual Liberation

The life and teachings of Mahavira, the 24th Tirthankara

Jainism is an ancient religion and philosophical tradition that originated in India. Its primary focus is on nonviolence, spiritual liberation, and ethical living. The most significant figure in Jainism is Mahavira, the 24th and last Tirthankara, a spiritual leader who attained enlightenment and guided others on the path to liberation. Mahavira, born as Vardhamana, lived during the 6th century BCE, and his teachings laid the foundation for the Jain tradition.

Mahavira's life story is filled with tales of asceticism, self-discipline, and spiritual insight. Born into a royal family, he renounced his worldly life at 30 to embark on a spiritual quest. For twelve years, he practised intense meditation, self-denial, and mortification of the flesh, ultimately attaining enlightenment, or Kevala Jnana, the highest form of spiritual realisation in Jainism.

As a Tirthankara, Mahavira dedicated the rest of his life to teaching others about the path to spiritual liberation. His teachings emphasised the importance of self-restraint, nonviolence, and compassion for all living beings. He also taught us the importance of understanding the interconnectedness of all things and the need to live in harmony with the world around us.

The foundational concepts: Ahimsa, Anekantavada, and Aparigraha

Three essential principles form the foundation of Jainism: Ahimsa, Anekantavada, and Aparigraha.

Ahimsa, or nonviolence, is the central tenet of Jainism. It is the practice of non-harming and non-injury, not just in physical actions but also in thoughts and words. Jainism teaches that all living beings possess a soul and are worthy of respect and compassion. This principle extends to all aspects of life, including diet, with Jains often following a strict vegetarian or vegan lifestyle.

Anekantavada, or the doctrine of many-sidedness, is a unique aspect of Jain philosophy. It emphasises human perception and understanding limitations, asserting that reality is multifaceted and that no single perspective can fully capture its complexity. Anekantavada encourages open-mindedness, tolerance, and the acceptance of multiple viewpoints, fostering intellectual humility and promoting harmony and understanding among different beliefs and perspectives.

Aparigraha, or non-attachment, is the principle of non-possession and detachment from material and emotional desires. Jainism teaches that excessive attachment to worldly possessions and relationships can hinder spiritual growth and lead to suffering. By practising Aparigraha, one can free oneself from the cycle of craving and attachment, cultivating contentment, simplicity, and inner peace.

The Jain ethical code and the path to spiritual liberation

The path to spiritual liberation in Jainism involves adhering to a strict ethical code based on the three aforementioned foundational principles. This ethical code is embodied in the Five Great Vows or Mahavratas, observed by both Jain monks and laypersons, albeit to varying degrees of strictness.

- **Ahimsa (nonviolence):** To practice nonviolence in thought, word, and deed and to cultivate compassion for all living beings.
- **Satya (truthfulness):** Always speak the truth and avoid dishonesty, deception, or falsehood.
- **Asteya (non-stealing):** To refrain from taking anything that has not been given freely or without permission and to respect the property and rights of others.
- **Brahmacharya (celibacy or chastity):** To practice sexual restraint and maintain the purity of mind and body. While monks practice complete celibacy, laypersons are expected to maintain fidelity within their marriages and exercise moderation in sexual matters.
- **Aparigraha (non-attachment):** To detach oneself from material possessions, relationships, and emotional desires, focusing on spiritual growth and inner contentment.

The practice of these vows, meditation, and self-reflection helps individuals progress on the path to spiritual liberation. The ultimate goal in Jainism is to attain Moksha, or liberation from the cycle of birth, death, and rebirth (samsara). By achieving Moksha, the soul is freed from the bondage of karma and attains a state of eternal bliss and knowledge, transcending the limitations of the material world.

The influence of Jainism on Indian culture and philosophical thought

Jainism has had a profound impact on Indian culture and philosophical thought, with its emphasis on nonviolence, tolerance, and compassion. Jainism's focus on Ahimsa has greatly influenced Indian society, contributing to the widespread practice of vegetarianism and respect for animal life. Moreover, the principle of Anekantavada has encouraged intellectual humility, dialogue, and acceptance of differing perspectives within the broader Indian philosophical tradition.

Jainism has also significantly contributed to Indian art, architecture, and literature. Many of India's most famous and beautifully adorned temples are Jain temples, showcasing the community's devotion to their spiritual beliefs and artistic expression. Jain literature encompasses a vast collection of sacred texts, poetry, and philosophical treatises, reflecting the rich intellectual heritage of the Jain tradition.

The impact of Jainism extends beyond the borders of India as well. Its teachings on nonviolence, compassion, and tolerance have resonated with individuals worldwide, leading to the establishment of Jain communities in various countries. The principles of Jainism have also influenced other spiritual and philosophical traditions, such as Buddhism, which shares similarities in its teachings on nonviolence, karma, and the pursuit of spiritual liberation.

In conclusion, Jainism is a deeply spiritual and ethical tradition that has shaped Indian culture and philosophical thought for thousands of years. Its nonviolence, tolerance, and detachment teachings inspire countless individuals on their path to spiritual liberation. Its rich intellectual heritage contributes to the ongoing exploration of life's most profound questions. As a heterodox school of Indian philosophy, Jainism provides a unique and valuable perspective on the nature of reality, ethics, and the pursuit of spiritual growth, demonstrating the diversity and richness of India's philosophical landscape.

Carvaka: The Materialist School of Indian Philosophy

The origins and development of Carvaka philosophy

Carvaka, also known as Lokayata, is an ancient Indian philosophical school that espouses materialism, scepticism, and hedonism. The origins of Carvaka philosophy can be traced back to the 7th century BCE. It is considered one of the heterodox schools of Indian philosophy due to its divergence from the Vedic tradition. Carvaka emerged during intense intellectual and spiritual exploration in India, where diverse philosophical perspectives were debated and refined.

The foundational text of Carvaka philosophy, the now-lost Barhaspatya Sutras, was authored by Brihaspati, a sage often regarded as the school's founder. Although the original text has not survived, its teachings have been preserved through quotations and critiques found in the works of other Indian philosophers. This allows modern scholars to piece together an understanding of Carvaka's core tenets and its place in the history of Indian philosophy.

The key concepts: materialism, scepticism, and hedonism

Materialism: At the heart of Carvaka philosophy is the belief in materialism, the idea that the material world is the only reality and that everything can be reduced to material entities and their interactions. Carvaka rejects the existence of non-material entities, such as the soul or consciousness, as independent of the body. The school maintains that the mind and consciousness are mere by-products of the physical body, specifically the arrangement of atoms within it.

Carvaka's materialist stance starkly contrasts the metaphysical and spiritual views of other Indian philosophical schools, which posit the existence of non-material realities such as Brahman, Atman, and the various realms of existence in Hindu cosmology.

Scepticism: Closely related to its materialist outlook, Carvaka embraces scepticism as a core aspect of its philosophical approach. The school is highly critical of supernatural claims, religious rituals, and the authority of sacred texts. It argues that knowledge should be derived from direct experience and empirical evidence rather than relying on scripture, tradition, or other sources of authority.

Carvaka is particularly critical of the Vedic tradition, dismissing the idea of an eternal, divine revelation and the efficacy of rituals and sacrifices. This sceptical stance extends to karma, reincarnation, and the afterlife, which Carvaka denies as unfounded beliefs that lack empirical evidence.

Hedonism: Carvaka's hedonistic philosophy emphasises the pursuit of pleasure and happiness as the primary goal in life. It asserts that sensory experiences and worldly enjoyment are the only sources of genuine happiness. Consequently, Carvaka dismisses asceticism, self-denial, and the pursuit of spiritual liberation as misguided endeavours that deprive individuals of the pleasures and happiness in the material world.

Carvaka's hedonistic approach is not without its moral and ethical dimensions. The school encourages its followers to live responsibly, respecting the rights and well-being of others while pursuing their happiness. Moreover, Carvaka acknowledges that unrestrained indulgence in pleasure can lead to suffering and negative consequences, advocating for a balanced and prudent approach to pursuing happiness.

The significance of Carvaka in the evolution of Indian thought

Although Carvaka did not gain widespread acceptance in India compared to other philosophical schools, its materialist, sceptical, and hedonistic perspectives have significantly impacted the evolution of Indian thought. Carvaka's critiques of the Vedic tradition and the authority of sacred texts fostered a spirit of intellectual inquiry and debate, encouraging other philosophical schools to refine and defend their positions.

Carvaka's emphasis on empirical evidence and direct experience as sources of knowledge contributed to the development of Indian epistemology and the diverse array of pramanas (means of knowledge) that characterise the various Indian philosophical schools.

Additionally, the materialist and hedonistic aspects of Carvaka philosophy provided a counterbalance to the more spiritual and metaphysical perspectives of other Indian philosophical schools. This diversity of thought allowed for a vibrant and dynamic intellectual climate in ancient India, where ideas were constantly challenged, debated, and refined.

Carvaka's lasting influence can be seen in later Indian philosophical developments, such as the emergence of materialist and atheistic strands within the broader Indian intellectual tradition. Furthermore, Carvaka's scepticism and insistence on empirical evidence have resonated with contemporary secular and rationalist movements in India and worldwide.

In conclusion, Carvaka occupies a unique and important position within the history of Indian philosophy. As a heterodox school that challenged the prevailing religious and metaphysical views of its time, Carvaka promoted intellectual inquiry, scepticism, and a focus on empirical evidence that enriched the Indian philosophical landscape. Its materialist, sceptical, and hedonistic perspectives provide a valuable counterpoint to more spiritual and metaphysical schools of thought, underscoring the richness and diversity of Indian philosophy.

The Interplay of the Heterodox Schools with Orthodox Schools

The commonalities and differences between heterodox and orthodox schools

The heterodox schools of Indian philosophy, which include Buddhism, Jainism, and Carvaka, diverge from the orthodox schools in several key respects. One of the main differences lies in their stance towards the Vedas and Vedic authority. While the six orthodox schools accept the Vedas as the ultimate source of knowledge and wisdom, the heterodox schools reject this claim and pursue their independent lines of inquiry.

Despite their differences, there are also significant commonalities between heterodox and orthodox schools. For instance, both are deeply concerned with understanding the nature of reality, the self, and the path to liberation. Additionally, many orthodox or heterodox schools have similar ethical concerns, such as pursuing a virtuous life and cultivating moral character.

The philosophical debates and mutual influences

Throughout the history of Indian philosophy, there have been numerous interactions and exchanges between the heterodox and orthodox schools, resulting in mutual influences and the development of new ideas. These philosophical debates spanned many topics, including metaphysics, epistemology, ethics, and logic.

For example, the development of the Nyaya school's logical and epistemological framework was significantly influenced by debates with Buddhist philosophers. In turn, the Buddhist school of thought adapted and refined many of its arguments in response to critiques from the orthodox schools. Similarly, the Jain concept of Anekantavada, which emphasises the multiplicity of perspectives and the limitations of human knowledge, has inspired both orthodox and heterodox thinkers in their quest to understand the complex nature of reality.

Another notable example of philosophical interaction can be found in the development of ethics. For instance, the emphasis on nonviolence (Ahimsa) in Jainism influenced both the orthodox and heterodox schools, leading to a broader acceptance of the principle of nonviolence in Indian thought. Additionally, the ethical teachings of Buddhism, such as the Eightfold Path and the concept of compassion, resonated with many orthodox thinkers who integrated these ideas into their systems of ethics.

The role of heterodox schools in shaping Indian intellectual history

The heterodox schools have played a pivotal role in shaping the intellectual landscape of India. Their contributions to Indian philosophy are significant in their own right, and how they have enriched and challenged the orthodox schools.

The heterodox schools have been instrumental in pushing the boundaries of philosophical inquiry, questioning established dogmas, and encouraging the development of new ideas. By challenging the authority of the Vedas and the orthodox schools, they promoted a spirit of critical inquiry and intellectual freedom that has been a hallmark of Indian thought. This spirit of questioning and exploration led to various philosophical systems, each with unique insights and perspectives on reality, knowledge, ethics, and the human condition.

Moreover, heterodox schools have significantly influenced India's cultural and social fabric. For example, Buddhism and Jainism, emphasising nonviolence, compassion, and ethical conduct, have shaped the moral values and social norms of Indian society. These religions also contributed to the growth of art, architecture, and literature, leaving a lasting impact on the cultural heritage of India.

The heterodox schools have also played a crucial role in the global spread of Indian philosophy. Buddhism, in particular, has profoundly impacted East and Southeast Asia's intellectual and spiritual traditions, influencing the development of various schools of thought in China, Japan, Korea, Tibet, and beyond. This widespread dissemination of Indian thought has fostered cross-cultural exchange and mutual understanding among diverse civilisations.

In conclusion, the interplay between the heterodox and orthodox schools of Indian philosophy has been a driving force in the evolution of Indian thought. By engaging in philosophical debates, challenging established dogmas, and forging new paths of inquiry, the heterodox schools have enriched the intellectual landscape of India and contributed to the development of a dynamic and diverse philosophical tradition. The mutual influences and exchanges between these schools have led to a rich tapestry of ideas and insights that continue to inform and inspire contemporary philosophical discussions and spiritual practice.

Moreover, heterodox schools have impacted India and the world's broader cultural, social, and intellectual history. Promoting values such as nonviolence, compassion, and ethical conduct helped shape the moral foundations of Indian society and contributed to the evolution of its cultural heritage. The global spread of Buddhism, in particular, has facilitated cross-cultural exchange and fostered a deeper understanding of the diverse philosophical traditions that have emerged from the Indian subcontinent.

In today's world, where the pursuit of knowledge, wisdom, and ethical living is more important than ever, the heterodox schools of Indian philosophy offer valuable insights and perspectives that can enrich our understanding of the human condition and help us navigate the complex challenges of modern life. As we continue to explore the depths of Indian philosophical thought, the contributions of heterodox schools will remain a vital source of inspiration and guidance for generations to come.

The Legacy of the Heterodox Schools

The enduring impact of Buddhism, Jainism, and Carvaka on Indian philosophy

The heterodox schools of Indian philosophy, namely Buddhism, Jainism, and Carvaka, have left an indelible mark on the intellectual landscape of India and beyond. Their unique perspectives on metaphysics, ethics, and spirituality have contributed to the rich diversity of Indian philosophical thought and shaped its development over millennia.

For instance, Buddhism introduced the Middle Way concept, emphasising the importance of moderation and balance in all aspects of life. This principle has had a lasting impact on Indian philosophy and has influenced the development of various schools of thought, including some orthodox systems like Vedanta. The Buddha's teachings on the Four Noble Truths and the Eightfold Path have provided a practical and accessible framework for spiritual practice that has resonated with people across cultures and eras.

Jainism, on the other hand, has made significant contributions to the ethical dimensions of Indian philosophy, particularly in its emphasis on Ahimsa (nonviolence), Anekantavada (the multiplicity of perspectives), and Aparigraha (non-attachment). Various philosophical schools in India have adopted and adapted these principles, reflecting the widespread influence of Jain thought on Indian culture and society. Furthermore, the Jain ethical code has provided a comprehensive and rigorous path to spiritual liberation, emphasising the importance of self-discipline, asceticism, and strict adherence to moral principles.

Carvaka, as a materialist and sceptical school, has played a crucial role in promoting critical thinking and challenging established religious and philosophical ideas in India. Although Carvaka did not survive as a distinct school of thought, its influence can be seen in the intellectual debates and discussions that have taken place throughout Indian history. The Carvaka emphasis on empirical evidence, scepticism, and hedonism has encouraged philosophers from other schools to engage with and refine their ideas in response to Carvaka critiques.

The global appeal and influence of heterodox ideas

The heterodox schools of Indian philosophy have not only impacted the intellectual landscape of India. Still, they have spread far and wide, leaving their mark on various cultures and civilisations worldwide. Buddhism, in particular, has profoundly influenced East and Southeast Asia's spiritual, philosophical, and artistic traditions. Its ideas have resonated with people in countries such as China, Japan, Korea, and Tibet, giving rise to unique schools of thought and cultural expressions.

Although not as widespread as Buddhism, Jainism has also found a global audience, particularly among diasporic Indian communities. Its ethical principles of nonviolence, respect for all living beings, and environmental consciousness have found a receptive audience in contemporary times as more people seek sustainable and compassionate ways of living.

Carvaka's materialist and sceptical ideas have also found resonance with modern secular and humanist movements, which emphasise critical thinking, rational inquiry, and a focus on human well-being rather than divine intervention. In this way, Carvaka's legacy continues to inform contemporary debates on the role of religion, spirituality, and ethics in human life.

The continued relevance of the heterodox schools in contemporary philosophical discussions and spiritual practice

The heterodox schools of Indian philosophy remain relevant today as historical curiosities and living traditions that continue to inspire philosophical inquiry and spiritual practice. Their ideas and perspectives offer valuable insights into the human condition, addressing fundamental questions about the nature of reality, the meaning of life, and the path to liberation.

Buddhism's emphasis on mindfulness, compassion, and the cultivation of inner peace has found a receptive audience in contemporary society, where individuals grapple with the challenges of modern life and seek solace in spiritual practices. The Buddha's teachings offer practical guidance on navigating the complexities of human existence and fostering mental and emotional well-being.

Jainism's focus on nonviolence, ecological awareness, and respect for all living beings has become increasingly relevant in a world grappling with environmental crises and social conflict. Its ethical principles offer a blueprint for sustainable living and promote harmony between humans and the natural world. Moreover, the Jain emphasis on Anekantavada, or the acceptance of multiple perspectives, provides a valuable lesson in tolerance and open-mindedness, particularly relevant in today's pluralistic societies.

Carvaka's scepticism and rationalism inspire critical thinking and intellectual inquiry in a world where dogma and superstition still sway. Its focus on empirical evidence and logical reasoning provides a solid foundation for scientific inquiry. At the same time, its hedonistic principles remind us of the importance of enjoying the pleasures of life in moderation.

In conclusion, the heterodox schools of Indian philosophy, with their distinctive approaches and ideas, have had a lasting impact on India's intellectual and spiritual landscape and beyond. Their continued relevance in contemporary philosophical discussions and spiritual practice demonstrates these ancient traditions' timeless wisdom and adaptability. As we face the challenges of the modern world, the insights offered by Buddhism, Jainism, and Carvaka can help us navigate the complexities of human existence and contribute to the evolution of human thought and culture.

Conclusion

The heterodox schools of Indian philosophy, namely Buddhism, Jainism, and Carvaka, represent diverse ideas and approaches to understanding the nature of reality, human existence, and the path to spiritual liberation. As we look back on the rich history of Indian thought, it becomes clear that these heterodox schools have contributed significantly to developing various intellectual traditions within India and across the globe. In this concluding section, we will explore the diversity and richness of these schools and underscore the importance of studying them for a comprehensive understanding of Indian thought.

The diversity and richness of the heterodox schools of Indian philosophy

The heterodox schools of Indian philosophy demonstrate a remarkable degree of diversity in their conceptual frameworks and methodologies. Buddhism, for instance, encompasses a wide range of philosophical perspectives, from the Theravada tradition's emphasis on individual enlightenment and the cultivation of mindfulness to the Mahayana tradition's focus on compassion, altruism, and the Bodhisattva ideal. With its esoteric practices and tantric techniques, the Vajrayana tradition further expands the scope of Buddhist thought and offers a distinctive path to spiritual awakening.

On the other hand, Jainism presents a unique system of thought rooted in the teachings of Mahavira, the 24th Tirthankara. With its emphasis on nonviolence (Ahimsa), the multiplicity of perspectives (Anekantavada), and non-attachment (Aparigraha), Jainism offers a distinctive ethical and spiritual framework that has resonated with countless seekers over the millennia. The Jain tradition also stands out for its rigorous ascetic practices and commitment to spiritual liberation through self-discipline and inner transformation.

Carvaka, the materialist school of Indian philosophy, represents another distinctive approach to understanding reality and human existence. With its focus on materialism, scepticism, and hedonism, Carvaka challenges many fundamental assumptions of orthodox and other heterodox schools. Though the Carvaka school did not survive as a distinct philosophical tradition, its influence can still be traced in various strands of Indian thought, particularly in scepticism and rational inquiry.

The importance of exploring the heterodox schools for a comprehensive understanding of Indian thought

Studying the heterodox schools of Indian philosophy is crucial for anyone seeking to understand India's intellectual and spiritual traditions. These schools, with their distinctive ideas and approaches, have significantly shaped the evolution of Indian thought and have left an indelible mark on the cultural and intellectual landscape of the subcontinent.

The heterodox schools have engaged in vibrant philosophical debates and exchanges with their orthodox counterparts, leading to a cross-pollination of ideas and various new schools of thought. By exploring the complex interplay between orthodox and heterodox schools, we can better appreciate the richness and dynamism of Indian philosophical inquiry.

Furthermore, heterodox schools have profoundly influenced India's broader cultural, artistic, and religious traditions and beyond. For instance, the spread of Buddhism throughout Asia has led to the emergence of diverse Buddhist art forms, architectural styles, and regional adaptations of Buddhist teachings. Likewise, Jainism has made significant contributions to Indian art, architecture, and literature, and its ethical principles have deeply influenced the moral fabric of Indian society.

In today's globalised world, the ideas and practices of heterodox schools continue to resonate with individuals from various cultural and religious backgrounds. The teachings of Buddhism and Jainism, in particular, have found a receptive audience among those seeking alternative spiritual paths and ethical frameworks for addressing contemporary social and environmental challenges.

In conclusion, the heterodox schools of Indian philosophy, with their diverse and innovative approaches to understanding reality and human existence, offer a rich and invaluable resource for anyone seeking to delve into the depths of Indian thought. The enduring legacy of Buddhism, Jainism, and Carvaka testifies to the intellectual vitality and spiritual wisdom that these traditions embody.

By engaging with the ideas and practices of these heterodox schools, we can gain a more comprehensive understanding of the multifaceted nature of Indian philosophy and appreciate the intricate tapestry of intellectual inquiry that has unfolded across the Indian subcontinent over the centuries. As we continue to explore and reflect on these heterodox schools, we may find inspiration, insight, and guidance for our philosophical and spiritual journeys, individually and collectively.

In the end, studying the heterodox schools of Indian philosophy not only enriches our knowledge of the vast and varied landscape of Indian thought but also opens up new avenues for dialogue, understanding, and mutual enrichment among different intellectual traditions and spiritual paths. The enduring appeal and relevance of the heterodox schools remind us of the timeless wisdom contained in these ancient teachings and their potential to inform and transform our contemporary perspectives on life, meaning, and the nature of reality.

As we grapple with the challenges and complexities of the modern world, the insights and ideas offered by the heterodox schools of Indian philosophy become all the more significant. They invite us to question our assumptions, broaden our horizons, and cultivate a spirit of open-minded inquiry and compassionate engagement with the world around us.

Moreover, heterodox schools can serve as a powerful reminder of the importance of intellectual diversity, the value of pluralistic approaches to understanding reality, and the need for respectful and constructive dialogue among different philosophical perspectives. By embracing the lessons and insights of heterodox schools, we can enrich our intellectual and spiritual pursuits, foster a deeper appreciation of the interconnectedness of all life, and cultivate a more just, compassionate, and sustainable world for future generations.

In essence, the exploration of the heterodox schools of Indian philosophy provides us with a unique opportunity to encounter the rich and diverse tapestry of Indian thought, appreciate its enduring legacy and global influence, and draw upon its timeless wisdom as we navigate the complexities and challenges of our own lives and the wider world. As we delve into the teachings of Buddhism, Jainism, and Carvaka, we are invited to embark on a journey of self-discovery, intellectual growth, and spiritual transformation. This journey has the potential to enrich our understanding of ourselves and our fellow human beings, and the world in which we live.

In an age marked by rapid technological advancements, growing environmental concerns, and the increasing interconnectedness of human societies, the heterodox schools of Indian philosophy can offer valuable insights and guidance on navigating these complex realities with wisdom, compassion, and a sense of responsibility. By engaging with the ideas and practices of these schools, we can not only deepen our understanding of Indian thought but also develop a more holistic, nuanced, and integrated perspective on the human condition and our place within the larger web of existence.

Ultimately, studying the heterodox schools of Indian philosophy is not merely an academic exercise but a transformative journey that invites us to question, reflect, and grow as we seek to understand and engage with the world. By embracing the rich diversity and wisdom of these schools, we can cultivate a spirit of intellectual curiosity, ethical discernment, and spiritual awakening that has the potential to enrich our lives, foster mutual understanding, and contribute to the flourishing of a more just, compassionate, and sustainable global community.

CHAPTER FIVE

The Philosophical Landscape of Indian Ethics and Aesthetics

Introduction to Indian Ethics and Aesthetics

Indian philosophical thought has long recognised the importance of ethics and aesthetics as essential components of human life and understanding. Over the centuries, various schools of thought have developed unique perspectives on ethical principles and artistic expression, contributing to a rich and diverse intellectual landscape encompassing orthodox and heterodox traditions. This chapter aims to provide an overview of the key themes, concepts, and ideas that have emerged from this vibrant philosophical milieu, offering insights into how Indian thinkers have grappled with questions of morality, beauty, and creativity.

The significance of ethics and aesthetics in Indian philosophical thought

Ethics and aesthetics play a central role in Indian philosophy, as they address fundamental questions about human nature, the nature of reality, and our place in the world. Ethics, or the study of moral values and principles, seeks to understand and articulate the guidelines that govern our actions, relationships, and decisions. Indian ethical thought encompasses a wide range of topics, from the nature of moral duty (dharma) and the goals of human life (purusharthas) to the cultivation of virtues and the development of moral character.

On the other hand, aesthetics is the branch of philosophy that deals with the nature of beauty, art, and taste and the creation and appreciation of artistic expressions. Indian aesthetics is deeply intertwined with religious, spiritual, and philosophical traditions, which have shaped how beauty and artistic value are understood and experienced. Indian thinkers have developed sophisticated theories and concepts related to the essence of beauty (rasa), the purpose and function of art, and the role of the artist and the audience in the creative process.

The exploration of moral values and artistic expression

Exploring moral values and artistic expression in Indian philosophy is vast and multifaceted—each philosophical school, whether orthodox or heterodox, has uniquely contributed to developing ethical and aesthetic thought. For instance, the Vedas and the Upanishads contain hymns, rituals, and philosophical speculations that lay the groundwork for later ethical and aesthetic theories. The Bhagavad Gita, a key text in the Hindu tradition, addresses the moral dilemmas the protagonist Arjuna faces while offering insights into the nature of dharma, karma, and spiritual practice.

The six orthodox schools of Indian philosophy contribute distinctively to human life's ethical and aesthetic dimensions. For example, the Yoga school emphasises the eight limbs of yoga and provides a systematic path for moral and spiritual development. Similarly, the Nyaya and Vaisheshika schools, with their rigorous logical and analytical frameworks, contribute to our understanding of ethical concepts and principles. With its dualistic metaphysics, the Sankhya school offers insights into the nature of consciousness and its role in ethical and aesthetic experience.

The Mimamsa school's focus on interpreting Vedic injunctions and rituals highlights the importance of ethical conduct in achieving spiritual goals. Lastly, the Vedanta school, with its rich metaphysical and ontological theories, provides a context for understanding the ultimate nature of reality and the ethical implications that arise from this understanding.

The heterodox schools of Indian philosophy also offer unique perspectives on ethics and aesthetics. Buddhism, emphasising the Four Noble Truths and the Eightfold Path, provides a moral framework grounded in compassion, mindfulness, and the pursuit of spiritual liberation. Jainism, with its emphasis on nonviolence (ahimsa), plurality of perspectives (anekantavada), and non-attachment (aparigraha), offers a distinctive ethical system that seeks to minimise harm and promote spiritual growth. The Carvaka school, with its materialist and hedonist outlook, challenges traditional ethical and aesthetic theories by advocating a focus on sensual pleasure and the enjoyment of life.

In addition to these philosophical schools, Indian thought has also produced a rich body of literature on aesthetics, such as the Natyashastra, a seminal treatise on the theory and practice of performing arts, which explores the nature of rasa (emotional essence) and the role of the artist and audience in the artistic experience. The concept of rasa is central to Indian aesthetics, as it captures the essence of beauty and the emotional impact of artistic expressions. Rasa theory has been widely applied to performing arts like dance, music, drama, visual arts, poetry, and literature.

Indian aesthetic thought has also been enriched by the contributions of great poets, playwrights, and artists, such as Kalidasa, considered one of the greatest classical Sanskrit poets and playwrights. His works, such as Abhijnanasakuntalam and Meghaduta, exemplify the heights of Indian literary and artistic expression, revealing deep insights into human emotions, desires, and experiences.

The interplay between ethics and aesthetics in Indian philosophy has produced a rich and diverse intellectual landscape that reflects India's unique cultural, religious, and historical contexts. As such, exploring the various ethical and aesthetic theories developed by the different philosophical schools can provide a more comprehensive understanding of Indian thought and its enduring legacy. Furthermore, the continued relevance of these ideas in contemporary philosophical discussions and spiritual practice highlights the universality and timeless nature of Indian ethical and aesthetic insights.

In conclusion, the diversity and richness of Indian ethics and aesthetics are testimony to the profound depth and complexity of Indian philosophical thought. By engaging with these ideas, we can better appreciate the intricate tapestry of ethical principles, artistic expressions, and cultural values that have shaped India's intellectual and spiritual heritage. The study of Indian ethics and aesthetics not only offers a window into the minds of the thinkers who have contributed to this rich tradition but also serves as a source of inspiration for contemporary philosophers, artists, and spiritual practitioners seeking to understand and address the moral and aesthetic dimensions of human life. The continued exploration of these ideas promises to yield valuable insights and contribute to the ongoing dialogue on the nature of morality, beauty, and human experience in a global context.

The Ethical Dimensions of Indian Philosophy

The ethical dimensions of Indian philosophy are multifaceted and deeply intertwined with its metaphysical and spiritual beliefs. From the ancient Vedas to the sophisticated systems of thought developed by the orthodox and heterodox schools, Indian philosophy has consistently emphasised the importance of ethical values and principles as central to understanding the human condition, the nature of reality, and the path to spiritual liberation. In this section, we will examine some of the key ethical concepts and teachings that have emerged from the rich tapestry of Indian philosophical thought, including the role of Dharma, Karma, and Moksha, the concept of Ahimsa (nonviolence) in Buddhism and Jainism, the ethical teachings of the Bhagavad Gita, and the moral frameworks of the various philosophical schools.

The role of Dharma, Karma, and Moksha in ethical thought

Dharma, Karma, and Moksha are three central concepts that underpin the ethical dimensions of Indian philosophy. Dharma, often called duty or righteousness, refers to the moral and ethical principles governing individual and social behaviour. It is the foundation of an individual's actions and determines the proper course of conduct based on one's caste, stage of life, and personal circumstances. Dharma emphasises the importance of living in harmony with the universe's natural order and fulfilling one's moral and social obligations.

Karma, which means action, is the law of cause and effect that governs the moral consequences of one's actions. According to the doctrine of Karma, every action has positive or negative consequences, which determine the nature of one's future experiences, both in this life and in subsequent lives. By performing good deeds and avoiding harmful actions, an individual can accumulate positive Karma, leading to a more favourable future.

Moksha, or spiritual liberation, is the ultimate goal of human life in many Indian philosophical systems. It represents a state of freedom from the cycle of birth, death, and rebirth (samsara) and the accompanying suffering. Pursuing Moksha is intricately linked to ethical conduct, as one's actions and the accumulation of Karma play a crucial role in determining the soul's progress towards liberation.

The concept of Ahimsa (nonviolence) in Buddhism and Jainism

Ahimsa, or nonviolence, is a core ethical principle in Buddhism and Jainism. It is the practice of refraining from causing harm or injury to any living being through physical actions, speech, or thought. Ahimsa is essential for spiritual progress and for cultivating compassion, empathy, and understanding in both traditions. The practice of Ahimsa extends not only to human beings but also to animals, plants, and the environment, as all living beings are considered interconnected and worthy of respect.

In Buddhism, the principle of Ahimsa is incorporated into the Five Precepts, which form the basic code of ethical conduct for laypeople. The first precept is the commitment to abstain from taking the life of any sentient being. The Buddha emphasised the importance of nonviolence as a crucial aspect of the path to enlightenment and taught that cultivating loving-kindness (Metta) and compassion (Karuna) were essential for spiritual development.

Jainism places an even greater emphasis on the practice of Ahimsa, making it the central tenet of its moral philosophy. The Jains believe that every living being has a soul and that causing harm or injury to any living being creates negative Karma, which hinders spiritual progress. Consequently, Jain monks and nuns adhere to strict codes of conduct to minimise harm to all living beings, including wearing a cloth over their mouths to avoid inhaling insects and carefully inspecting their paths to avoid stepping on small creatures.

The ethical teachings of the Bhagavad Gita

The Bhagavad Gita, a revered Hindu scripture, presents a profound exploration of ethics, duty, and the nature of the self. Set on the battlefield of Kurukshetra, the Gita is a dialogue between Prince Arjuna and the god Krishna, who serves as his charioteer and spiritual guide. The text grapples with human existence's dilemmas and moral complexities and offers guidance on navigating these challenges while adhering to one's Dharma.

One of the central teachings of the Bhagavad Gita is the concept of Nishkama Karma or selfless action. According to this doctrine, one should perform one's duties without attachment to the fruits or outcomes of one's actions. By relinquishing the desire for personal gain and acting in accordance with Dharma, an individual can break free from the bonds of Karma and attain spiritual liberation.

The Gita also emphasises the importance of cultivating virtues such as discipline, detachment, and devotion, which are essential for spiritual growth and self-realisation. Furthermore, it introduces the concept of the three Gunas (Sattva, Rajas, and Tamas), which are qualities that influence human behaviour and mental states. By cultivating Sattva (purity, balance) and reducing the influence of Rajas (passion, activity) and Tamas (ignorance, inertia), an individual can achieve greater clarity, wisdom, and inner peace.

The moral frameworks of the various philosophical schools

Each of the major Indian philosophical schools has developed its moral framework, often based on Dharma, Karma, and Moksha concepts. These frameworks guide how to lead a righteous life and attain spiritual liberation.

In orthodox schools, such as Samkhya and Yoga, the focus is on spiritual discipline and the purification of the mind to attain Moksha. For example, the Yoga Sutras of Patanjali outlines the eightfold path of Yoga, which includes ethical principles such as Yamas (restraints) and Niyamas (observances) as essential steps towards self-realisation.

The Mimamsa school emphasises the performance of Vedic rituals and the correct interpretation of the sacred texts. For the Mimamsakas, adherence to Dharma is essential for attaining a favourable afterlife and eventual spiritual liberation.

The Vedanta school, particularly the Advaita Vedanta, emphasises the importance of self-inquiry, meditation, and the cultivation of wisdom to realise the true nature of the self (Atman) and its identity with the ultimate reality (Brahman). According to Advaita Vedanta, realising this non-dual truth is the key to attaining Moksha.

In heterodox schools, ethical frameworks often differ from orthodox schools, though they still share some common ground. As previously discussed, Buddhism emphasises the Four Noble Truths and the Eightfold Path as the way to end suffering and attain enlightenment. Its moral teachings revolve around cultivating wisdom, ethical conduct, and mental discipline.

Jainism, as mentioned earlier, emphasises Ahimsa and the observance of strict ethical codes to minimise harm to all living beings. Jains believe adhering to these principles can purify their souls and attain spiritual liberation (Kevala Jnana).

The materialist Carvaka school, on the other hand, rejects the concepts of Dharma, Karma, and Moksha, advocating instead for a more hedonistic approach to life. According to Carvaka philosophy, pursuing pleasure and avoiding pain are the primary goals of human existence. While this school does not provide a comprehensive ethical framework like the other schools, it does challenge some of the prevailing assumptions in Indian philosophical thought and encourages critical inquiry and scepticism.

In conclusion, Indian philosophy presents a diverse and rich array of ethical teachings and frameworks that have evolved over millennia. By examining these different systems of thought, one can gain valuable insights into the various ways human beings have sought to understand the nature of morality, the purpose of life, and the path to spiritual liberation. The ethical dimensions of Indian philosophy offer guidance for living a righteous life and provide a foundation for exploring more profound questions about the nature of reality, the self, and the ultimate meaning of existence. As a result, the study of Indian ethics can contribute significantly to a comprehensive understanding of Indian thought and broader philosophical and spiritual inquiries that transcend cultural and geographical boundaries.

The Indian Aesthetic Tradition

The origins and development of Indian aesthetics

Indian aesthetics can be traced back to the Vedic period, where the artistic expressions of the time were closely linked to sacred rituals and religious ceremonies. The beauty and creativity of the hymns, chants, and rituals provided an early basis for developing Indian aesthetic thought. As Indian society and culture evolved, so did its artistic and aesthetic traditions, resulting in various visual and performing art forms, including sculpture, painting, dance, music, and drama.

The Natyashastra, a treatise on performing arts authored by the sage Bharata Muni, is considered one of the foundational texts in Indian aesthetics. This extensive work, dating back to 200 BCE and 200 CE, covers various aspects of dance, music, and drama, including their theory, practice, and emotional impact. The treatise also discusses the broader philosophical aspects of aesthetics, laying the groundwork for developing a rich and sophisticated tradition of Indian artistic thought.

The concept of Rasa (aesthetic experience) in classical Indian literature and art

Rasa, loosely translated as "essence" or "taste," is a central concept in Indian aesthetics. It refers to the emotional experience evoked in the audience or the beholder by an artistic expression, whether in literature, music, dance, or visual arts. The Natyashastra identifies eight primary Rasas: love (Shringara), laughter (Hasya), sorrow (Karuna), anger (Raudra), courage (Veera), fear (Bhayanaka), disgust (Bibhatsa), and wonder (Adbhuta). Later, a ninth Rasa, peace (Shanta), was added to the list by aesthetician Abhinavagupta.

The idea of Rasa lies at the heart of Indian aesthetics, as it emphasises the importance of the emotional impact and the capacity of art to evoke a rich, immersive experience for its audience. This focus on the experiential aspect of art differentiates Indian aesthetics from some Western aesthetic traditions, which place a greater emphasis on the formal qualities of artistic expression.

The principles of Dhvani (suggestion) and Alankara (ornamentation)

Two other significant concepts in Indian aesthetics are Dhvani and Alankara. Dhvani, which means "sound" or "echo," refers to the power of suggestion in artistic expression. It encompasses the subtle, implied meanings and the layers of interpretation that can be derived from a work of art. Dhvani plays a crucial role in Indian poetry and literature, where the use of metaphor, symbolism, and allusion creates an intricate tapestry of meanings, evoking a rich aesthetic experience for the reader.

Alankara, which means "ornament" or "decoration," refers to the stylistic devices and embellishments artists employ to enhance their creations' beauty, charm, and appeal. Alankara encompasses many poetic literary devices, such as simile, metaphor, alliteration, and wordplay. In the visual arts, Alankara includes intricate patterns, designs, motifs, and the skilful manipulation of colour, form, and composition. Alankara refers to the intricate rhythms, melodies, and choreographic patterns that enrich the performance in music and dance.

The interplay between aesthetics and spirituality

In Indian thought, aesthetics and spirituality are deeply intertwined, with artistic expression often serving as a means of exploring and expressing spiritual themes, emotions, and insights. This connection is evident in the prevalence of religious and mythological themes in Indian art, literature, and performing arts, which often seek to convey profound spiritual truths and evoke a sense of the divine.

The concept of Rasa, focusing on art's emotional and experiential dimensions, also highlights the spiritual aspects of aesthetics. The experience of Rasa can be seen as a form of transcendence, allowing the audience to connect with the deeper aspects of human experience and, in some cases, even with the divine. Many Indian classical art forms, such as Bharatanatyam and Kathakali dance, are deeply rooted in spirituality and are often performed as acts of devotion or worship.

The interplay between aesthetics and spirituality also manifests in India's numerous temples, sacred sites, and religious art. The sculptures, frescoes, and architectural designs of these sacred spaces not only showcase the artistic mastery of their creators but also serve as a visual representation of spiritual beliefs, concepts, and narratives.

In conclusion, Indian aesthetics is a rich and multifaceted tradition encompassing various artistic forms and philosophical ideas. The central concepts of Rasa, Dhvani, and Alankara and the strong connection between aesthetics and spirituality contribute to a unique and vibrant aesthetic tradition that continues to shape and inform India's artistic and cultural landscape. As we explore the ethical and aesthetic dimensions of Indian philosophy, we gain a deeper appreciation for the complexity, depth, and beauty of Indian thought and artistic expression.

The Intersection of Ethics and Aesthetics in Indian Philosophy

The pursuit of beauty, truth, and goodness

In Indian philosophy, the pursuit of beauty, truth, and goodness are deeply interconnected, reflecting the holistic nature of Indian thought. The concept of Satyam, Shivam, Sundaram, which translates to "Truth, Goodness, and Beauty," exemplifies this connection. Indian thinkers have long held that these three ideals are interdependent and mutually reinforcing. Pursuing truth and understanding reality is the foundation of ethical conduct, allowing individuals to make informed decisions about their actions and consequences. Likewise, appreciating beauty in the natural world and human creations is believed to uplift the human spirit and inspire ethical behaviour.

The connections between moral values and artistic expression

The interconnectedness of ethics and aesthetics in Indian philosophy is also evident in the close relationship between moral values and artistic expression. Classical Indian art, literature, and performing arts often embody and convey ethical principles, stories, and teachings, serving as vehicles for moral education and spiritual growth. Many traditional Indian art forms, such as dance, music, and theatre, have their roots in religious or spiritual contexts. Their primary function is to convey moral lessons, illustrate spiritual principles, or evoke devotion.

For example, the Indian classical dance form of Bharatanatyam originates in Hindu temple dances and seeks to convey stories from Hindu mythology and spirituality. Through its intricate and expressive movements, Bharatanatyam entertains and educates the audience about the moral values and ethical principles embedded in the stories it portrays.

Similarly, Indian classical music, such as the Hindustani and Carnatic traditions, has a deep spiritual foundation. Its performance often aims to induce a meditative state or facilitate a connection with the divine. The lyrics of many compositions in Indian classical music are based on sacred texts or convey moral and spiritual messages, reinforcing the connection between aesthetics and ethics.

The role of art and literature in promoting ethical and spiritual growth

Indian philosophy posits that art and literature are crucial in promoting ethical and spiritual growth. This idea is rooted in the belief that aesthetic experiences, such as appreciating beauty in nature or enjoying a well-crafted poem, can elevate the human spirit and inspire individuals to lead a more virtuous life.

In Indian aesthetics, the concept of Rasa plays a significant role in promoting ethical and spiritual growth. Rasa refers to the emotional or aesthetic experience evoked in the audience by an artistic work, and the ability of the work to convey deep emotions and spiritual experiences is considered central to its value. A work of art that successfully evokes Rasa can lead the audience towards a state of spiritual elevation and moral refinement.

Indian literature, particularly the epics such as the Ramayana and the Mahabharata, is a rich source of ethical teachings and moral lessons. These epics depict the struggles and triumphs of heroes and heroines, presenting complex moral dilemmas and illustrating the consequences of their choices. Through these narratives, readers can explore and internalise the ethical principles and values that underpin Indian society.

The connection between ethics and aesthetics in Indian philosophy is also evident in the role of artistic expression in religious and spiritual practices. In Hinduism, for example, the creation and veneration of sacred images, known as murtis, serve as a means to cultivate devotion, invoke the divine presence, and facilitate the spiritual growth of the worshipper. Similarly, reciting sacred texts or performing devotional music can inspire ethical and spiritual reflection, fostering a deeper understanding of the values and principles that guide one's life.

In conclusion, the Indian philosophical tradition demonstrates a profound interplay between ethics and aesthetics, with both domains deeply intertwined and mutually reinforcing. The pursuit of beauty, truth, and goodness and the connections between moral values and artistic expression are essential aspects of Indian thought. By exploring these intersections, we can better understand India's cultural and intellectual heritage and appreciate the depth and diversity of Indian philosophical ideas. Furthermore, this holistic approach to understanding the relationship between ethics and aesthetics offers valuable insights for contemporary discussions on the role of art and literature in fostering moral and spiritual growth. As we engage with the timeless wisdom of Indian philosophy, we are reminded of the potential of art to uplift the human spirit, inspire ethical conduct, and contribute to the overall well-being of individuals and societies.

The Influence of Indian Ethics and Aesthetics on Culture and Society

The impact of ethical thought on Indian social structures and institutions

The ethical thought of India has left a profound impact on various aspects of its culture and society. The Indian ethical systems, deeply rooted in diverse philosophical traditions, have shaped the development of social structures and institutions throughout history. For instance, the concept of Dharma (duty, righteousness) has been a guiding force in establishing social norms and regulating interpersonal relationships. Dharma emphasises the importance of fulfilling one's duties and responsibilities toward family, community, and society, thereby promoting social harmony and cooperation.

The principle of Ahimsa (nonviolence), a central tenet in Buddhism and Jainism, has also had a lasting influence on Indian society. This principle extends beyond the mere absence of physical violence to encompass a broader philosophy of compassion, tolerance, and respect for all living beings. As a result, vegetarianism has become widespread in India, and the protection of animals has been enshrined in various social and religious customs.

Karma (the law of cause and effect) and Moksha (spiritual liberation) are other essential concepts that have permeated Indian ethical thought. The belief in karma has fostered a sense of moral accountability, encouraging individuals to strive for righteous actions and avoid harmful deeds. The pursuit of Moksha, on the other hand, has motivated countless people to engage in spiritual practices and seek inner transformation, reinforcing the ethical foundations of Indian society.

The contributions of Indian aesthetics to classical arts, architecture, and literature

Indian aesthetics has profoundly influenced the development of classical arts, architecture, and literature. The Indian aesthetic tradition has its roots in the Vedic period, with the Rigveda and other sacred texts providing glimpses into the early artistic expressions and sensibilities of the Indian people. Over time, these aesthetic ideas evolved and expanded, giving rise to a rich artistic heritage that includes music, dance, painting, sculpture, and architecture.

The concept of Rasa (aesthetic experience) has been central to developing classical Indian arts. Rasa refers to the emotional essence or taste that an artist seeks to evoke in the audience, and it forms the basis of various artistic genres and styles. In Indian classical dance, for instance, the Natya Shastra, an ancient performing arts treatise, outlines the various Rasas and their corresponding emotional states, guiding dancers in their quest to evoke these emotions through their performances.

Similarly, the principles of Dhvani (suggestion) and Alankara (ornamentation) have significantly influenced Indian literature and poetry. Dhvani emphasises the power of suggestion in poetic expression, allowing readers to derive multiple layers of meaning from a single verse. Alankara, on the other hand, refers to using figurative language and poetic devices to enhance the beauty and impact of literary works.

Indian aesthetics has also left an indelible mark on architecture, with numerous examples of magnificent temples, palaces, and other structures showcasing their creators' intricate craftsmanship and artistic vision. The principles of Vastu Shastra, an ancient science of architecture, have guided the design and construction of these architectural marvels, ensuring harmony with nature and the surrounding environment.

The enduring legacy of Indian ethical and aesthetic ideas in contemporary culture

The enduring legacy of Indian ethical and aesthetic ideas in contemporary culture is a testament to the profound influence and adaptability of Indian thought. Spanning millennia, Indian philosophy has not only shaped the cultural and spiritual fabric of the Indian subcontinent but has also made significant contributions to global intellectual and artistic traditions. As the world becomes increasingly interconnected, the ethical and aesthetic ideas embedded in Indian philosophy resonate and inspire contemporary culture, offering valuable insights for addressing modern challenges and enriching the human experience.

One of the most notable aspects of Indian ethical thought is its emphasis on the interconnectedness of all living beings and the need for compassion, empathy, and nonviolence (ahimsa) in our interactions with others. This ethical framework has inspired contemporary movements advocating social justice, environmental conservation, and animal rights. The principles of karma and dharma, which emphasise the importance of ethical action and personal responsibility, have also found resonance in modern spiritual and self-help teachings, encouraging individuals to lead morally grounded and purposeful lives.

Aesthetically, Indian culture has significantly impacted various forms of contemporary art, design, and fashion. The intricate patterns, vibrant colours, and symbolic motifs characteristic of Indian textiles, jewellery, and architecture have been widely adopted and reinterpreted by artists and designers worldwide. Moreover, Indian classical dance and music, with their rich and complex expressive vocabulary, have inspired and influenced numerous contemporary performers and composers. Bollywood, India's thriving film industry, has gained global recognition and popularity, introducing Indian aesthetics and storytelling traditions to a broader audience.

Indian literature and poetry have also had a lasting impact on contemporary culture. Ancient Indian epics, such as the Mahabharata and Ramayana, continue to be retold and adapted in various forms, reflecting the timeless appeal of their narratives, themes, and characters. The mystical and philosophical verses of poets like Kabir, Mirabai, and Tagore have been translated into multiple languages, offering readers a wealth of inspiration and wisdom worldwide.

The influence of Indian ethical and aesthetic ideas can also be seen in the West's growing popularity of practices such as yoga, meditation, and Ayurveda. These holistic systems emphasise the need for inner harmony, balance, and well-being, addressing the mind, body, and spirit. As more people seek alternatives to materialistic and stress-driven lifestyles, Indian philosophies offer a valuable and enduring source of inspiration for cultivating a more mindful, compassionate, and fulfilling existence.

Conclusion

The richness and diversity of Indian ethics and aesthetics

The world of Indian philosophy is incredibly diverse and rich in both its ethical and aesthetic dimensions. The ethical principles that have emerged from various schools of thought, such as Dharma, Karma, and Moksha, have profoundly impacted the moral fabric of Indian society. Similarly, the aesthetic principles of Rasa, Dhvani, and Alankara have provided a solid foundation for Indian art, literature, and architecture. This diversity is a testament to the depth of India's cultural and intellectual heritage.

Throughout the history of Indian thought, philosophy's ethical and aesthetic dimensions have been intertwined, giving rise to a unique and holistic approach to understanding the human experience. The ethical teachings of various philosophical schools have shaped the moral outlook of the Indian people. At the same time, the aesthetic traditions have contributed to developing a vibrant artistic landscape.

The importance of understanding the ethical and aesthetic dimensions of Indian philosophy

Given the depth and breadth of Indian philosophy, it is crucial to appreciate and engage with its ethical and aesthetic dimensions to gain a comprehensive understanding of Indian thought. By examining these dimensions, we can better understand the historical and cultural contexts that have shaped the development of Indian philosophical thought.

Furthermore, engaging with the ethical and aesthetic dimensions of Indian philosophy allows us to appreciate the interconnectedness of the various schools of thought. While heterodox and orthodox schools may differ in their fundamental principles and approaches, they often share common ground regarding ethical and aesthetic matters. This interconnectedness reflects the inherent unity and diversity of Indian thought and demonstrates the value of studying the various schools in tandem.

The potential for Indian ethical and aesthetic thought to enrich the global philosophical and artistic discourse

Indian ethics and aesthetics have much to offer to the global philosophical and artistic discourse. The unique perspectives and insights provided by the various schools of thought can contribute significantly to our understanding of the human experience and inform and inspire contemporary ethical and aesthetic discussions.

The ethical teachings of Indian philosophy, such as Dharma, Karma, and Ahimsa, can provide valuable guidance for addressing modern moral dilemmas and navigating the complexities of contemporary life. Similarly, the aesthetic principles of Rasa, Dhvani, and Alankara can offer fresh perspectives on art, literature, and beauty and serve as a source of inspiration for artists and scholars alike.

In conclusion, the ethical and aesthetic dimensions of Indian philosophy reflect the richness and diversity of Indian thought. By engaging with these dimensions, we can better understand the historical and cultural contexts that have shaped Indian intellectual tradition. Furthermore, the unique insights and perspectives offered by Indian ethics and aesthetics have the potential to enrich global philosophical and artistic discourse, contributing to a more nuanced and holistic understanding of the human experience.

CHAPTER SIX

The Intersection of Philosophy and Science in India

Introduction to Philosophy and Science in India

The significance of scientific inquiry in Indian philosophical thought

Indian philosophy is concerned with metaphysical and ethical questions and has a long-standing tradition of scientific inquiry. The Indian philosophical schools have made significant contributions to various fields of science, such as mathematics, astronomy, medicine, and linguistics. This deep-rooted interest in scientific inquiry reflects the holistic nature of Indian thought, where empirical knowledge and metaphysical concepts are seen as complementary and interdependent.

Pursuing scientific knowledge has been an integral part of Indian intellectual tradition, with various philosophical schools embracing the empirical method to gain a deeper understanding of the natural world. This empirical approach has enabled the development of sophisticated knowledge systems and contributed to the growth of various scientific disciplines in India.

The integration of empirical knowledge and metaphysical concepts

One of the distinctive features of Indian philosophy is its ability to integrate empirical knowledge with metaphysical concepts. This integration reflects the inherent unity of Indian thought, where the material and the spiritual realms are seen as interconnected and mutually dependent.

The various schools of Indian philosophy have made significant efforts to incorporate scientific knowledge into their metaphysical frameworks. For instance, the Vaisheshika school, focusing on atomism and particularity, has developed a comprehensive understanding of the physical world, seamlessly integrated into its broader metaphysical system. Similarly, the Sankhya school's dualist framework, which posits the existence of Purusha (consciousness) and Prakriti (matter), incorporates a detailed account of the natural world and the process of evolution.

The integration of empirical knowledge and metaphysical concepts in Indian philosophy is also evident in the development of various scientific disciplines. For example, the field of Ayurveda, an ancient system of medicine, is deeply rooted in the philosophical teachings of Indian schools. The principles of Ayurveda draw upon understanding the natural world, the metaphysical concepts of the three doshas (biological energies) and the interconnectedness of body, mind, and spirit.

Another example is the field of Indian astronomy, which has a long history of observational and theoretical advancements. The astronomers of ancient India were able to make accurate predictions and calculations by combining empirical observations with a profound understanding of the cosmological principles derived from the philosophical schools. This integration of empirical knowledge and metaphysical concepts allowed Indian astronomers to develop a sophisticated understanding of celestial phenomena, which has had a lasting impact on the field of astronomy.

Moreover, the field of linguistics in ancient India was heavily influenced by the philosophical insights of various schools, particularly the Mimamsa and the Vedanta. The Indian grammarians, such as Panini and Patanjali, developed comprehensive language and grammar theories deeply rooted in philosophical principles. These theories have profoundly impacted the development of linguistics as a scientific discipline, both in India and around the world.

In conclusion, the intersection of philosophy and science in India reflects the holistic and integrated nature of Indian thought. The various schools of Indian philosophy have made significant contributions to the development of scientific knowledge, and their empirical insights have been seamlessly incorporated into the metaphysical frameworks. This integration of empirical knowledge and metaphysical concepts has allowed Indian philosophy to develop a comprehensive understanding of the natural world and make lasting contributions to various scientific disciplines.

Mathematics in Ancient India

The development of Indian mathematics and its connection to philosophy

Mathematics in ancient India has a rich history and was closely connected to philosophical thought. Indian mathematicians and philosophers recognised the importance of numbers and geometry in understanding the universe and its underlying principles. They believed studying mathematics would deepen their comprehension of the cosmos and its inherent order. Consequently, they developed various mathematical concepts and techniques that have significantly contributed to the field of mathematics.

The early development of Indian mathematics can be traced back to the Vedic period, during which mathematics was primarily used for religious and astronomical purposes. The Sulba Sutras, composed around 800-500 BCE, contain the earliest known Indian mathematical texts. These texts focus on the construction of fire altars and provide geometrical rules and measurements, showcasing the practical applications of mathematics in religious rituals.

The contributions of Indian mathematicians, such as Aryabhata and Brahmagupta

Several prominent Indian mathematicians have made significant contributions to the field of mathematics. One such mathematician was Aryabhata, who lived around 476-550 CE. Aryabhata's work, Aryabhatiya, is a seminal text in Indian mathematics and astronomy. It contains important concepts such as the approximation of pi, the introduction of the sine function, and the solution of linear and quadratic equations. Aryabhata also contributed to trigonometry and established methods for calculating the areas and volumes of various geometric shapes.

Another influential Indian mathematician was Brahmagupta, who lived during the 7th century CE. His most important work, the Brahmasphutasiddhanta, contains significant advancements in algebra and arithmetic. Brahmagupta introduced the concept of negative numbers and zero, which played a crucial role in the development of modern arithmetic. He also devised methods for solving indeterminate equations and developed the first-known formula for computing the area of a cyclic quadrilateral.

The impact of Indian mathematics on global scientific history

The mathematical contributions of ancient India have had a profound impact on global scientific history. Indian mathematicians introduced fundamental concepts widely used in modern mathematics, such as the decimal system and zero and negative numbers. These innovations were transmitted to the Islamic world and later to Europe, contributing to the development of the global mathematical tradition.

Indian mathematics also influenced other fields of science, such as astronomy and engineering. The trigonometric functions and geometrical techniques developed by Indian mathematicians were utilised to make accurate astronomical observations and predictions. These discoveries were later incorporated into the work of Islamic and European astronomers, contributing to the growth of global astronomical knowledge.

Furthermore, Indian mathematics provided a solid foundation for developing architectural and engineering marvels throughout the Indian subcontinent. The precise calculations and geometrical principles used in constructing ancient temples, forts, and palaces are a testament to the advanced mathematical understanding of Indian architects and engineers.

In conclusion, the development of mathematics in ancient India was deeply intertwined with philosophical thought, and Indian mathematicians made significant contributions to the field. Their discoveries, such as the decimal system, trigonometric functions, and the concept of zero, have impacted global scientific history. The legacy of Indian mathematics continues to influence modern scientific endeavours and serves as a reminder of the rich intellectual heritage of ancient India.

Astronomy and Astrology in Indian Philosophy

The origins and growth of Indian astronomy and astrology

The origins of Indian astronomy and astrology can be traced back to the Vedic period, which spans from 1500 BCE to 500 BCE. During this time, the Vedas, the sacred texts of Hinduism, made numerous references to celestial phenomena, such as the position of stars and planets, eclipses, and the solstices. This early interest in celestial events was primarily driven by the need to establish a precise calendar for religious rituals and agricultural activities. As a result, Indian astronomy and astrology developed alongside each other, with astronomical observations providing the basis for astrological predictions.

Over time, the study of astronomy and astrology evolved into a more systematic and sophisticated discipline. Indian astronomers developed mathematical techniques to measure and predict celestial phenomena, compiled in texts such as the Surya Siddhanta and the Siddhantas of Varahamihira. These works laid the foundation for Indian astronomy and astrology as we know it today.

The significance of astronomical observations in Indian philosophical schools

Astronomy played a significant role in shaping Indian philosophical thought. Many Indian philosophical schools incorporated astronomical observations into their understanding of the universe and its underlying principles. For instance, the Sankhya and Vaisheshika schools recognised the importance of time and space in understanding the cosmos. They used astronomical observations to establish their theories of cosmic cycles and atomic structures.

Furthermore, astronomical knowledge was essential for developing the Indian calendar and determining the timing of religious rituals and ceremonies. The accurate measurement of time allowed Indian philosophers to contemplate the nature of time and explore its relationship with human existence and consciousness.

In addition to its impact on metaphysical thought, astronomy also influenced practical aspects of Indian philosophy. Astrology, closely linked to astronomy, was crucial in guiding marriage, career, and health decisions. Indian philosophers acknowledged the significance of celestial events in shaping human destiny and sought to understand the influence of the cosmos on individual lives.

The influence of Indian astronomy on other cultures and civilisations

Indian astronomy and astrology have considerably impacted other cultures and civilisations throughout history. As early as the 5th century CE, Indian astronomical knowledge was transmitted to the Sasanian Empire in Persia. This knowledge was later adopted by Islamic scholars, who translated Indian astronomical texts into Arabic during the Golden Age of Islam. These Arabic translations were subsequently introduced to Europe, contributing to the development of European astronomy and astrology.

Indian astronomy also profoundly influenced the East, particularly in China and Southeast Asia. Indian astronomical concepts, such as the lunar mansions and planetary periods, were integrated into Chinese and Southeast Asian astronomical systems. Additionally, Indian astrological ideas and practices were assimilated into the local cultures, shaping their respective astrological traditions.

In conclusion, astronomy and astrology have played a significant role in developing Indian philosophy. The study of celestial phenomena has influenced metaphysical thought, practical decision-making, and the establishment of a precise calendar system. The legacy of Indian astronomy and astrology extends beyond the Indian subcontinent. Various cultures and civilisations have adopted and adapted its ideas and techniques throughout history, highlighting the global importance and impact of Indian astronomical knowledge.

Medicine and Indian Philosophy

The foundation and evolution of Ayurveda, the ancient Indian system of medicine

Ayurveda, the ancient Indian system of medicine has its roots in the Vedic period, dating back to around 1500 BCE.'Ayurveda' is derived from the Sanskrit words 'ayur,' meaning life, and 'veda,' meaning knowledge or science. Thus, Ayurveda can be understood as the science of life. The primary texts of Ayurveda, the Charaka Samhita, the Sushruta Samhita, and the Ashtanga Hridayam, were compiled between the 6th century BCE and the 7th century CE. These texts encompass a vast body of medical knowledge, covering diagnosis, treatment, pharmacology, surgery, and preventive care.

Ayurveda evolved, integrating new knowledge and innovations from various sources, including ancient Indian philosophical schools. As a result, Ayurveda developed into a holistic system of medicine that emphasises the interconnection between body, mind, and spirit in maintaining health and well-being.

The integration of philosophy, medicine, and spirituality in Ayurvedic practices

Ayurveda's holistic approach to health and healing is rooted in the Indian philosophical tradition. The system recognises the importance of balance among the three fundamental bodily energies or doshas (Vata, Pitta, and Kapha) derived from the five elements (earth, water, fire, air, and space). Imbalances in these doshas are believed to cause various ailments, and Ayurvedic treatments aim to restore balance through dietary modifications, herbal remedies, and lifestyle practices.

In addition to focusing on physical health, Ayurveda also addresses well-being's mental and spiritual dimensions. This is exemplified by the concept of Sattva, Rajas, and Tamas, representing the three qualities of the mind. Ayurvedic practitioners emphasise the cultivation of sattvic qualities (purity, harmony, and clarity) to promote mental and emotional health. Meditation, yoga, and other spiritual practices are often prescribed alongside medical treatments to foster holistic healing.

The contributions of Indian philosophers to the understanding of human anatomy and physiology

Indian philosophers made significant contributions to understanding human anatomy and physiology, which were incorporated into the Ayurvedic system of medicine. The Sushruta Samhita, attributed to the ancient surgeon Sushruta, provides a detailed account of human anatomy, including descriptions of organs, blood vessels, nerves, and bones. This text also outlines surgical procedures, instruments, and techniques, showcasing the advanced surgical knowledge of ancient Indian physicians.

Another important contribution of Indian philosophers to medicine is the concept of Prana or life force. This vital energy, which flows through subtle channels called nadis, is believed responsible for maintaining the body's physiological processes. Indian philosophers recognised the importance of regulating the flow of Prana through practices such as yoga, pranayama (breath control), and meditation to maintain health and well-being.

In conclusion, Indian philosophy profoundly impacted the development of medicine in ancient India. The Ayurvedic system of medicine embodies the holistic approach to health and healing characteristic of Indian philosophical thought. Ayurveda has provided a comprehensive framework for understanding and treating the human body and mind by integrating philosophy, medicine, and spirituality. The contributions of Indian philosophers to the understanding of human anatomy and physiology have shaped Ayurveda's development and enriched the global history of medical knowledge.

The Scientific Approach of Ancient Indian Philosophers

The emphasis on observation, experimentation, and logical reasoning

Ancient Indian philosophers demonstrated a strong commitment to scientific inquiry by emphasising the importance of observation, experimentation, and logical reasoning. The philosophical schools of India, both orthodox and heterodox, adopted a systematic and rigorous approach to knowledge acquisition. The Nyaya school, for instance, developed a sophisticated system of logic and epistemology that laid the foundation for scientific inquiry in India. The Nyaya school's epistemological framework identified four valid sources of knowledge: perception, inference, analogy, and testimony.

Observation and direct experience were highly valued in ancient Indian thought. The empirical observation was considered a reliable source of knowledge, leading to the development of various sciences, including astronomy, mathematics and medicine. Experimentation was crucial in advancing these fields, with practitioners refining their methods and theories based on empirical evidence.

The interdisciplinary nature of Indian philosophical and scientific inquiry

One of the distinguishing features of ancient Indian philosophical and scientific inquiry was its interdisciplinary nature. Indian philosophers recognised the interconnectedness of various fields of knowledge and often drew from multiple disciplines to develop a comprehensive understanding of the world.

For example, the study of mathematics was closely linked to astronomy and astrology, as mathematical concepts were used to develop accurate models of celestial phenomena. Similarly, medicine, yoga, and spirituality were intricately connected, with physicians drawing on philosophical concepts to inform their understanding of human health and well-being.

This interdisciplinary approach also facilitated the cross-pollination of ideas between different schools of thought. Philosophers from various schools often engaged in debates and discussions, challenging each other's theories and refining their own in response. This intellectual exchange helped advance the understanding of various scientific disciplines and enriched the overall philosophical knowledge.

The legacy of Indian scientific thought in later Indian intellectual traditions

The legacy of Indian scientific thought in later Indian intellectual traditions is a testament to the ingenuity, curiosity, and intellectual prowess of ancient Indian scholars. Indian scientific achievements span various fields, including mathematics, astronomy, medicine, and metallurgy. These accomplishments have laid the foundation for later Indian intellectual traditions and significantly influenced scientific thought development in the modern era.

Mathematics is one domain where Indian scientists made groundbreaking contributions. The concept of zero, the decimal system, and positional notation can all be traced back to ancient Indian mathematicians such as Aryabhata and Brahmagupta. Their work laid the foundation for later Indian scholars like Bhaskaracharya, whose contributions to algebra and trigonometry further enriched the mathematical tradition. These mathematical concepts and techniques were later adopted and adapted by the Islamic world, eventually making their way to Europe and shaping the development of modern mathematics.

In astronomy, Indian scholars like Aryabhata and Varahamihira significantly advanced in understanding planetary motion, lunar and solar eclipses, and celestial coordinates. These insights informed the work of later Indian astronomers, who refined their predecessors' models and calculations. Their sophisticated understanding of astronomy also contributed to the development of the Indian calendar and the accurate prediction of auspicious dates for religious and cultural events.

Ayurveda, the ancient Indian system of medicine, is another area where Indian scientific thought has had a lasting impact. Rooted in the knowledge of herbs, plants, and natural remedies, Ayurveda emphasises the importance of maintaining a balance between the mind, body, and spirit. The foundational texts of Ayurveda, the Charaka Samhita and Sushruta Samhita, continue to be studied and revered by practitioners today. Furthermore, Ayurvedic principles and practices have inspired modern approaches to holistic health and well-being, with increasing global interest in using natural remedies and preventive medicine.

Indian metallurgical knowledge and craftsmanship, particularly in producing high-quality steel known as wootz, has had a lasting impact on the development of metallurgy and engineering worldwide. Wootz steel was highly sought for its strength, durability, and beauty, with the famed Damascus steel swords made from Indian wootz. Indian metallurgical expertise laid the groundwork for later innovations in metallurgy and materials science, paving the way for the development of modern steel-making processes.

The Relevance of Indian Philosophy and Science in Today's World

The resurgence of interest in Indian scientific contributions

In recent years, there has been a resurgence of interest in Indian scientific contributions, both within India and internationally. Scholars and researchers increasingly recognise the significance of ancient Indian thought in shaping the development of various scientific disciplines, including mathematics, astronomy, and medicine. The works of prominent Indian mathematicians like Aryabhata and Brahmagupta are studied for their groundbreaking contributions to fields such as algebra, trigonometry, and the concept of zero. Similarly, the insights of Indian astronomers and the precision of their astronomical calculations have sparked renewed interest in the study of Indian astronomy.

This resurgence of interest is not limited to historical research but extends to the contemporary application of ancient Indian knowledge. For example, Ayurveda, the traditional Indian system of medicine, is gaining global recognition for its holistic approach to health and well-being. Its principles, based on the balance of body, mind, and spirit, are increasingly relevant in a world grappling with the challenges of modern lifestyles and chronic health conditions.

The applicability of ancient wisdom to modern scientific challenges

Ancient Indian wisdom has much to offer in addressing modern scientific challenges. Indian philosophical thought, emphasising logical reasoning, observation, and experimentation, provides a solid foundation for scientific inquiry. Additionally, the interdisciplinary nature of Indian philosophy encourages a holistic approach to problem-solving, which can be highly valuable in tackling the complex issues facing today's world.

For instance, the concept of sustainability and ecological balance, central to Indian philosophical thought, can be applied to address environmental challenges such as climate change and biodiversity loss. The principle of Ahimsa (nonviolence) in Jainism and Buddhism can inspire ethical considerations in biotechnology and artificial intelligence, encouraging responsible innovation that respects the sanctity of life.

The ancient Indian yoga practice emphasises mental and physical well-being and has been embraced globally to combat stress, improve mental health, and promote overall wellness. The teachings of the Bhagavad Gita on selfless action and detachment from outcomes provide valuable guidance for modern individuals seeking meaning and purpose amid the pressures of materialism and consumerism.

The potential for Indian philosophy and science to foster innovation and global understanding

Indian philosophy and science have the potential to foster innovation and global understanding by providing fresh perspectives on enduring questions and promoting cross-cultural dialogue. The interdisciplinary nature of Indian thought encourages collaboration between researchers from different fields, spurring innovation and exchanging ideas.

Moreover, Indian philosophy's holistic approach can contribute to a more inclusive and nuanced understanding of global issues. By exploring the connections between ethics, aesthetics, science, and spirituality, Indian thought can offer valuable insights into the human experience, fostering empathy and understanding among people from diverse backgrounds and cultures.

In conclusion, the relevance of Indian philosophy and science in today's world is evident in the resurgence of interest in Indian scientific contributions and the applicability of ancient wisdom to modern challenges. By embracing the interdisciplinary and holistic approach of Indian thought, we can foster innovation, global understanding, and sustainable solutions to the world's complex issues.

Conclusion

The interconnectedness of philosophy and science in Indian thought

Throughout the history of Indian philosophy, the interconnectedness of philosophy and science has played a crucial role in shaping the evolution of thought. Indian philosophers have always valued empirical knowledge and logical reasoning, recognising the significance of scientific inquiry in understanding the world and the human experience. This emphasis on integrating empirical knowledge and metaphysical concepts has given rise to a rich tradition of intellectual inquiry that spans various disciplines, such as mathematics, astronomy, medicine, and ethics.

Indian philosophical thought reflects the belief that knowledge of the natural world and understanding metaphysical truths are complementary rather than contradictory. This holistic approach encourages the pursuit of knowledge in multiple domains and fosters intellectual curiosity, leading to groundbreaking discoveries and innovations.

The importance of exploring the scientific dimensions of Indian philosophy

Exploring the scientific dimensions of Indian philosophy is essential for a comprehensive understanding of the depth and breadth of Indian thought. By examining how Indian philosophers have engaged with scientific inquiry, we can gain valuable insights into the development of various scientific disciplines and appreciate the contributions made by Indian thinkers.

Moreover, studying scientific dimensions in Indian philosophy enables us to appreciate the interdisciplinary nature of Indian thought and its ability to address complex issues by integrating multiple perspectives. This can inspire contemporary researchers, who increasingly recognise the importance of interdisciplinary approaches in solving modern challenges.

Exploring the scientific aspects of Indian philosophy also sheds light on the historical context in which these ideas were developed, allowing us better to appreciate the intellectual achievements of ancient Indian thinkers. It can also inspire a renewed appreciation for the scientific legacy of India and promote a greater awareness of the global impact of Indian intellectual contributions.

The potential for Indian philosophical and scientific ideas to enrich global intellectual discourse and scientific progress

Indian philosophical and scientific ideas have much to offer in enriching global intellectual discourse and promoting scientific progress. The holistic and interdisciplinary approach of Indian thought encourages the pursuit of knowledge across various domains, fostering innovation and the exchange of ideas between different fields. By embracing this approach, researchers can break down the barriers between disciplines and facilitate greater collaboration and cross-pollination of ideas.

Additionally, Indian philosophical and scientific ideas can contribute to a more inclusive and nuanced understanding of global issues by offering alternative perspectives on enduring questions. By incorporating the insights of Indian thought into global intellectual discourse, we can promote greater understanding and empathy among people from diverse backgrounds and cultures, fostering a more inclusive and harmonious world.

The potential for Indian philosophical and scientific ideas to enrich global intellectual discourse and scientific progress is immense. By exploring the interconnectedness of philosophy and science in Indian thought, we can better appreciate the richness and diversity of Indian intellectual heritage. This can inspire new ways of thinking and problem-solving, ultimately contributing to a more comprehensive understanding of the world and the human experience.

In conclusion, the interconnectedness of philosophy and science in Indian thought highlights the importance of exploring the scientific dimensions of Indian philosophy. By delving deeper into the rich tradition of Indian thought, we can foster a greater appreciation for the unique contributions of Indian philosophers and scientists throughout history.

The Role of Indian Philosophy in Spiritual Practice

Introduction to Indian Philosophy and Spiritual Practice

The connection between philosophical thought and spiritual development in India

Indian philosophy has always been deeply intertwined with spiritual development. It seeks to answer fundamental questions about the nature of reality, the purpose of life, and the path to self-realisation. The various schools of Indian philosophy, orthodox and heterodox, have developed unique approaches to understanding the human experience, emphasising the importance of inner transformation and spiritual growth.

Philosophical thought in India has traditionally been seen as a means of exploring and understanding the deeper aspects of life, transcending the limitations of the material world, and attaining a state of inner peace and harmony. Indian philosophers have developed sophisticated frameworks for understanding the mind, consciousness, and the ultimate nature of reality, serving as the foundation for various spiritual practices and traditions.

The exploration of inner transformation and self-realisation

Pursuing inner transformation and self-realisation is a central theme in Indian philosophical thought. Many Indian philosophical schools, such as Vedanta, Yoga, Buddhism, and Jainism, emphasise the importance of self-knowledge, self-discipline, and self-transcendence to achieve spiritual liberation or enlightenment.

Self-knowledge: Indian philosophers have long recognised the importance of self-knowledge in inner transformation. By understanding the true nature of the self, one can gain insight into the workings of the mind and the nature of reality, ultimately transcending the cycle of suffering and ignorance. In the Upanishads, the quest for self-knowledge is portrayed as the highest form of wisdom, revealing the essential unity of the individual self (Atman) with the ultimate reality (Brahman).

Self-discipline: The cultivation of self-discipline is another key aspect of spiritual practice in Indian philosophy. This can take various forms, such as adherence to moral and ethical principles, the practice of meditation, and the observance of physical and mental austerities. In the Yoga tradition, for example, the eightfold path of Ashtanga Yoga outlines a comprehensive system for self-discipline, encompassing ethical principles (Yama and Niyama), physical postures (Asana), breath control (Pranayama), sensory withdrawal (Pratyahara), concentration (Dharana), meditation (Dhyana), and ultimately, the state of union with the divine (Samadhi).

Self-transcendence: The ultimate goal of many Indian philosophical traditions is to attain a state of self-transcendence, in which the individual transcends the limitations of the ego and experiences a profound sense of oneness with the universe. This can be achieved through various means, such as meditation, contemplation, self-inquiry, or devotion to a higher power. In the Bhagavad Gita, for instance, Lord Krishna teaches Arjuna the importance of self-transcendence through selfless action (Karma Yoga), knowledge (Jnana Yoga), and devotion (Bhakti Yoga).

Exploring inner transformation and self-realisation in Indian philosophy is deeply connected to pursuing spiritual growth and enlightenment. Individuals can progress toward spiritual liberation and attain a deeper understanding of themselves and the world around them by engaging in practices that cultivate self-knowledge, self-discipline, and self-transcendence.

In conclusion, the role of Indian philosophy in spiritual practice is significant and multifaceted, offering valuable insights into the process of inner transformation and self-realisation. The connection between philosophical thought and spiritual development in India highlights the importance of pursuing knowledge and understanding to achieve personal growth and spiritual liberation. Through exploring these themes, Indian philosophy provides a rich and diverse framework for spiritual practice. It offers guidance and inspiration to those seeking to cultivate a deeper sense of meaning, purpose, and connection.

Meditation and Mindfulness in Indian Philosophy

The role of meditation in various Indian philosophical traditions

Meditation has been integral to many Indian philosophical traditions for thousands of years. It is a practice that aims to bring about mental and emotional balance, self-awareness, and, ultimately, self-realisation. Meditation techniques vary across different philosophical schools but share the goal of developing inner peace, tranquillity, and heightened consciousness.

In the Yoga tradition, meditation is a crucial component of the eightfold path of Ashtanga Yoga. It is essential for achieving the ultimate goal of union with the divine, or Samadhi. Yoga emphasises the importance of focusing the mind and developing concentration through various meditation techniques.

In Vedanta, meditation is used as a means of self-inquiry, aimed at realising the true nature of the self (Atman) and its identity with the ultimate reality (Brahman). Through introspection and contemplation, practitioners seek to dissolve the illusion of separateness and attain a state of non-dual awareness.

In Buddhism, meditation is central to cultivating mindfulness and developing insight into the true nature of reality. The practice of meditation in Buddhism takes various forms, such as Vipassana (insight meditation), which focuses on the cultivation of awareness and understanding, and Samatha (concentration meditation), which emphasises the development of mental tranquillity and concentration.

The techniques and benefits of mindfulness and concentration

Techniques: Mindfulness and concentration techniques in Indian philosophy involve various practices to cultivate mental focus, self-awareness, and inner tranquillity. Some common techniques include focusing on the breath, body sensations, thoughts, emotions, or visualisations. By maintaining attention to a chosen object or sensation, practitioners develop greater mental stability and clarity, leading to a deeper understanding of themselves and their experiences.

Benefits: The benefits of mindfulness and concentration practices in Indian philosophy are numerous and wide-ranging. They include increased mental clarity, emotional balance, stress reduction, and enhanced well-being. Additionally, these practices can lead to greater self-awareness, self-control, and a deeper understanding of the nature of reality. By cultivating mindfulness and concentration, individuals can develop the capacity to navigate life's challenges with greater equanimity and wisdom.

The influence of Indian meditation practices on global spiritual practices

Indian meditation practices have had a significant and lasting impact on spiritual traditions worldwide. In recent decades, there has been a surge of interest in meditation and mindfulness techniques in the West, resulting in the adoption and adaptation of Indian practices by various spiritual and secular communities.

The spread of Buddhist meditation practices, such as Vipassana and Zen, has been instrumental in popularising mindfulness meditation in Western societies. These practices have been incorporated into various therapeutic approaches, such as Mindfulness-Based Stress Reduction (MBSR) and Mindfulness-Based Cognitive Therapy (MBCT), which have gained widespread recognition for their effectiveness in promoting mental well-being and resilience.

The teachings of Indian gurus and spiritual masters, such as Swami Vivekananda, Paramahansa Yogananda, and Maharishi Mahesh Yogi, have also played a vital role in introducing meditation practices to the Western world. Their teachings have inspired the development of numerous meditation and yoga centres, retreats, and training programs, making these practices accessible to a broader audience.

The influence of Indian meditation practices extends beyond religious and spiritual contexts. They have also found a place in secular settings, such as schools, corporations, and healthcare institutions, where mindfulness and meditation are increasingly recognised as valuable tools for fostering emotional balance, mental clarity, and overall well-being.

Interfaith dialogue and the convergence of spiritual traditions have further contributed to the global reach of Indian meditation practices. The encounter between different faiths has facilitated sharing of ideas and practices, leading to the mutual enrichment of spiritual resources. This exchange has helped to create a more inclusive and diverse spiritual landscape in which Indian meditation techniques have gained prominence.

The digital age has also played a significant role in disseminating Indian meditation practices. The internet, social media, and mobile apps have made it easier than ever to access information and resources related to meditation, allowing individuals worldwide to explore and engage with these practices. This widespread accessibility has contributed to the growing popularity of meditation and mindfulness techniques within and outside traditional spiritual contexts.

Scientific research on the effects of meditation has further bolstered the global interest in Indian meditation practices. Numerous studies have demonstrated the benefits of meditation on various aspects of mental and physical health, such as stress reduction, improved focus, emotional regulation, and enhanced immune function. This empirical evidence has helped to legitimise meditation as a valuable tool for personal development and well-being, making it more appealing to individuals from diverse backgrounds and belief systems.

In summary, the influence of Indian meditation practices on global spiritual practices is multifaceted and far-reaching. Through the exchange of ideas, interfaith dialogue, technological advancements, and scientific research, these practices have become integral to the contemporary spiritual landscape, offering valuable tools for personal growth and self-discovery.

In conclusion, Indian meditation practices have profoundly impacted global spiritual practices, transcending cultural and geographical boundaries. The widespread adoption of these practices in various contexts demonstrates the universal appeal of Indian meditation techniques and their potential to enhance human well-being and self-awareness.

Yoga and Its Philosophical Foundations

Yoga, a millennia-old practice in ancient India, has garnered significant attention and respect worldwide for its spiritual, mental, and physical benefits. As a holistic system encompassing philosophy and practical techniques, yoga has profoundly influenced and enriched the lives of countless individuals in their pursuit of personal transformation and self-realisation.

The origins and development of yoga as a spiritual practice

The origins of yoga can be traced back to the pre-Vedic period, with early references found in the ancient texts of the Upanishads and the Bhagavad Gita. Yoga is often considered a spiritual discipline that aims to unite the individual self with the divine or absolute reality, transcending the limitations of the physical and mental world.

The practice of yoga evolved over centuries, integrating various aspects of Indian philosophical and spiritual thought. The ascetic practices of early yogis, such as meditation, breath control, and ethical disciplines, laid the foundation for the comprehensive system of yoga that exists today.

Over time, different schools of yoga emerged, each emphasising specific techniques and approaches to spiritual growth. These schools have contributed to the richness and diversity of the yoga tradition, making it accessible to individuals with varying interests and inclinations.

The philosophical basis of yoga in the Yoga Sutras of Patanjali

The Yoga Sutras of Patanjali, a seminal text in Indian philosophy, is considered the cornerstone of classical yoga philosophy. The text comprises 196 aphorisms that outline the principles and practices of Raja Yoga, a systematic approach to spiritual growth and self-realisation.

Patanjali's Yoga Sutras introduce the concept of the "eight limbs" of yoga (Ashtanga Yoga), which includes ethical disciplines (Yamas and Niyamas), postures (Asanas), breath control (Pranayama), sensory withdrawal (Pratyahara), concentration (Dharana), meditation (Dhyana), and ultimate absorption in the self (Samadhi). These eight limbs serve as a practical roadmap for individuals on their spiritual journey, guiding them towards self-realisation.

Patanjali's Yoga Sutras emphasise overcoming the fluctuations of the mind (chitta vrittis) to achieve a state of inner stillness and self-realisation. By practising the eight limbs of yoga, individuals can cultivate mental clarity, self-discipline, and inner peace, ultimately experiencing a profound sense of unity with the divine.

The different paths of yoga and their significance in spiritual growth

In addition to the classical Raja Yoga outlined in Patanjali's Yoga Sutras, several other paths of yoga have emerged over the centuries, each emphasising different aspects of spiritual practice. These paths include:

Karma Yoga: The path of selfless action, focusing on performing one's duties without attachment to the fruits of one's actions. This path teaches individuals to cultivate detachment, selflessness, and equanimity in facing life's challenges.

Bhakti Yoga: The path of devotion and love for the divine fosters emotional connection and surrender to a higher power. Individuals develop a deep sense of love, compassion, and humility through prayer, worship, and other devotional practices.

Jnana Yoga: The path of knowledge and wisdom, which emphasises self-inquiry, intellectual discernment, and philosophical reflection. By cultivating a deep understanding of the nature of reality, individuals can pierce through the veil of illusion (Maya) and recognize their true, divine nature.

Hatha Yoga: A system of physical postures, breathing techniques, and energy practices designed to purify the body, balance the subtle energy channels (nadis), and awaken the latent spiritual energy (kundalini). Hatha Yoga is a foundation for many modern yoga styles and is often practised in conjunction with other paths to support spiritual growth.

The different paths of yoga, while distinct in their approaches and techniques, ultimately share the same goal of spiritual growth and self-realisation. By engaging in one or more of these paths, individuals can cultivate a holistic approach to spirituality, integrating their physical, mental, and emotional dimensions to pursue inner transformation.

The Bhakti Movement: Devotion and Divine Love

The history and development of the Bhakti movement in India

The Bhakti movement, which originated in South India around the 7th century CE, has played a significant role in shaping India's religious and spiritual landscape. It emerged as a response to the dominance of the Brahminical orthodoxy and the rigid caste system. Bhakti emphasised the importance of devotion and personal experience over ritualism and caste-based hierarchy. This movement democratised spirituality, making it accessible to people of all social strata.

The Bhakti movement gained momentum between the 12th and 17th centuries as it spread across various regions of India. Many saint-poets and mystics, such as Kabir, Meera Bai, Surdas, and Tulsidas, championed the Bhakti philosophy and contributed to its growth. They composed devotional poetry and songs in vernacular languages, which allowed people to connect with the divine in their own languages and cultural contexts.

The philosophical foundations of Bhakti in the Bhagavad Gita and other texts

The philosophical foundations of Bhakti can be traced back to the Bhagavad Gita, a central text of Indian philosophy. The Gita presents three primary paths to spiritual liberation: Karma Yoga (the path of selfless action), Jnana Yoga (the path of knowledge), and Bhakti Yoga (the path of devotion). Bhakti Yoga emphasises cultivating a personal relationship with the divine through love, surrender, and devotion.

Bhakti philosophy also draws from the Puranas, a Hindu text genre that narrates the stories of gods and goddesses. The Puranas, such as the Bhagavata Purana, extol the virtues of devotion and divine love as the highest form of spiritual practice. Additionally, the devotional poetry of the Alvars and Nayanars, early Tamil poet-saints from South India, played a crucial role in shaping the Bhakti tradition.

The role of devotion, divine love, and surrender in spiritual practice

In the Bhakti tradition, devotion (bhakti) is the central aspect of spiritual practice. It is the means to attain a deep, personal connection with the divine, transcending the limitations of the ego and the material world. Devotees express their love and adoration for the divine through various forms, such as singing hymns, reciting mantras, and worshipping.

Divine love (prema) is considered the highest form of devotion. It is an intense, selfless love that seeks union with the divine. This love arises from recognising that the individual soul (jivatma) is inherently connected to the supreme soul (paramatma). Through divine love, devotees strive to dissolve the barriers that separate them from the divine, realising their true nature as one with the ultimate reality.

Surrender (prapatti) is another key aspect of Bhakti practice. It involves relinquishing control and entrusting oneself completely to the divine will. This surrender is both an acknowledgement of one's limitations and a profound expression of trust in the divine. Through surrender, devotees cultivate humility and develop unwavering faith in the divine's guidance and protection.

In conclusion, the Bhakti movement has played a significant role in shaping the spiritual landscape of India. It has democratised spirituality, making it accessible to people of all social backgrounds, and emphasised the importance of devotion, divine love, and surrender in spiritual practice. The philosophical foundations of Bhakti can be traced back to the Bhagavad Gita, the Puranas, and the devotional poetry of the Alvars and Nayanars. By fostering a personal relationship with the divine through love and surrender, the Bhakti tradition has enriched the lives of countless individuals and contributed to the diversity and richness of Indian spiritual practices.

The Spiritual Significance of Rituals in Indian Philosophy

In Indian philosophy, rituals are vital in spiritual practice and in cultivating a deeper understanding of reality. They serve as a bridge between the mundane and the sacred, allowing individuals to connect with the divine and experience spiritual growth.

The meaning and purpose of rituals in Indian thought

Rituals in Indian thought encompass a wide range of practices, including prayer, offering, meditation, and various rites and ceremonies. They are often seen as a means of attaining spiritual purity, transforming the individual, and maintaining cosmic order. Rituals can be performed for various purposes, such as seeking the blessings of the divine, expressing gratitude, requesting protection, or fulfilling specific spiritual goals.

In Indian philosophy, rituals are not viewed as mechanical actions but are imbued with profound meaning and significance. They are believed to facilitate the transformation of the practitioner's consciousness, aligning them with the cosmic order and bringing them closer to the ultimate reality. This transformative power of rituals is based on the concept of "ritual efficacy," which posits that the proper performance of a ritual can produce desired outcomes in the material and spiritual realms.

The connection between ritual practice and spiritual development in various philosophical schools

In the various philosophical schools of India, rituals are considered an essential component of spiritual practice. In the Vedic tradition, rituals are central to maintaining the cosmic order (Rta) and ensuring the well-being of individuals and society. The performance of rituals, such as yajnas (sacrificial ceremonies), is believed to foster a connection with the divine and bring about spiritual progress.

In the Upanishadic tradition, rituals are integrated with the quest for self-realisation and the knowledge of the ultimate reality (Brahman). They serve as a means of purifying the mind and preparing the individual to attain spiritual wisdom. For example, the Sandhyavandanam ritual, performed at the junctures of the day, helps the practitioner maintain a constant awareness of the divine and cultivates mindfulness.

In the context of the six orthodox schools of Indian philosophy, ritual practice plays a significant role in shaping an individual's spiritual journey. In the Mimamsa school, rituals are central to understanding the nature of dharma and the proper conduct of life. The Yoga school emphasises the importance of rituals to purify the mind and prepare it for yoga, ultimately leading to spiritual liberation.

The heterodox schools of Indian philosophy, such as Buddhism and Jainism, also emphasise the role of rituals in spiritual practice. In Buddhism, the practice of rituals, such as taking refuge in the Triple Gem (Buddha, Dharma, and Sangha), helps to reinforce the practitioner's commitment to the Buddhist path. In Jainism, rituals such as penance and fasting help cultivate self-discipline and nonviolence (ahimsa), critical aspects of Jain spiritual practice.

The role of symbolism and sacredness in Indian rituals

Symbolism and sacredness are central to the understanding of rituals in Indian philosophy. Rituals often involve symbols representing specific spiritual concepts, such as the mandala in tantric rituals, the sacred fire in Vedic yajnas, or the use of mudras (symbolic hand gestures) in various spiritual practices.

These symbols serve as a means of connecting the practitioner with deeper layers of meaning and reality, facilitating their spiritual transformation. The sacredness of rituals lies in their ability to create a bridge between the mundane world and the divine, allowing practitioners to transcend their ordinary state of consciousness and experience a sense of the sacred.

The performance of rituals often involves invoking deities or other spiritual beings, reciting sacred texts, and using ritual objects, such as incense, flowers, and offerings. These elements help create an atmosphere of sanctity and reverence, reinforcing the practitioner's connection with the divine.

Furthermore, rituals often follow a specific structure, sequence, and set of rules, which imbue them with a sense of order and harmony, mirroring the cosmic order they are designed to maintain. This structured approach to rituals also serves to discipline the mind and foster concentration, essential aspects of spiritual growth.

In conclusion, the role of rituals in Indian philosophy is multifaceted, encompassing various aspects of spiritual practice, from the purification of the mind to the attainment of self-realisation and spiritual liberation. The study of Indian rituals offers valuable insights into the intricate connections between philosophy, spirituality, and daily life, highlighting the profound wisdom and rich heritage of Indian thought. By understanding the significance of rituals in Indian philosophy, we can appreciate their potential to enrich our spiritual practices and deepen our connection with the divine.

Mantras and the Power of Sound in Indian Philosophy

The significance of mantras in Indian spiritual practice

Mantras, sacred sound formulas or syllables, play a vital role in Indian spiritual practice. They are considered powerful tools for spiritual transformation, unlocking higher states of consciousness and bringing about deep inner change. Mantras are an essential component of various Indian philosophical traditions, including Hinduism, Buddhism, and Jainism, and are used in meditation, rituals, and as part of daily spiritual practice.

Mantras are often composed of Sanskrit syllables, each of which is believed to possess a unique vibrational quality that can profoundly affect the practitioner's mental, emotional, and spiritual state. They can be as short as a single syllable, such as "Om," or as long as an entire verse from a sacred text. By repeating a mantra, either silently or aloud, practitioners can attune themselves to the specific energy and vibrations of the mantra, which can help facilitate spiritual growth, healing, and personal transformation.

The philosophical basis for the use of sacred sound and vibration

The use of mantras in Indian philosophy is rooted in the ancient Vedic concept of "Shabda Brahman" or "Nada Brahman," which posits that the entire universe is composed of sound vibrations. According to this concept, the physical world merely manifests the underlying cosmic sound or vibration, which gives rise to all forms of matter and energy.

The idea of sound as the primary creative force in the universe is also supported by the concept of the "Spanda Principle," a key tenet of Kashmir Shaivism, which asserts that the universe is in a constant state of subtle vibration or pulsation and that this vibration is the source of all creation and consciousness.

In Indian philosophical thought, the sacred sounds of mantras are believed to have the power to tap into these cosmic vibrations, allowing practitioners to align themselves with the fundamental energies of the universe. The repetition of mantras is said to create specific vibrational patterns in the mind and body, which can lead to the awakening of spiritual faculties, the purification of the subtle energy channels, and the attainment of higher states of consciousness.

The impact of mantras on consciousness and spiritual growth

The practice of mantra recitation and meditation is believed to have a transformative effect on the practitioner's consciousness. It helps to quiet the mind, cultivate mindfulness, and deepen one's connection with the divine. By focusing the mind on repeating a sacred sound or syllable, practitioners can gradually dissolve mental distractions, negative thought patterns, and emotional disturbances, allowing them to experience inner peace, clarity, and spiritual insight.

Mantras also play a significant role in spiritual growth, as they can facilitate awakening one's latent spiritual potential and help remove obstacles on the path to self-realisation. In many Indian philosophical traditions, mantra meditation is seen as an essential means of attaining spiritual liberation, as it enables practitioners to transcend the limitations of the ego and experience a state of unity with the divine.

Furthermore, the vibrations produced by mantra recitation are believed to purify the subtle energy channels within the body, known as nadis in the yogic tradition. This purification process can lead to the activation of the Kundalini energy, a powerful spiritual force that is said to reside at the base of the spine. When awakened, the Kundalini energy can rise through the various energy centres, or chakras, ultimately culminating in the crown chakra at the top of the head. This Kundalini awakening process is often associated with profound spiritual experiences, including heightened states of awareness, expanded consciousness, and deep insights into the nature of reality.

Moreover, mantra meditation can foster a deep sense of devotion and divine love, further facilitating spiritual growth and transformation. By engaging in the heartfelt repetition of a mantra, practitioners can cultivate a loving connection with the divine, which can serve as a powerful catalyst for inner change and the development of spiritual qualities, such as compassion, wisdom, and inner strength.

In conclusion, mantras play a crucial role in Indian spiritual practice and philosophy, connecting with the universe's fundamental energies, purifying the mind and body, and fostering spiritual growth and transformation. As sacred sound vibrations, mantras possess the potential to unlock higher states of consciousness and facilitate deep inner change, making them an invaluable tool for those seeking to explore the depths of their spiritual nature and attain self-realisation.

The Role of Ethics and Morality in Spiritual Practice

The connection between ethical behaviour and spiritual progress in Indian thought

The connection between ethical behaviour and spiritual progress has long been recognised in Indian philosophical thought, with various schools emphasising the importance of cultivating moral virtues as a prerequisite for spiritual growth and self-realisation. Indian philosophy has always been deeply concerned with the nature of the human condition and how individuals can attain lasting happiness and fulfilment. This quest for self-understanding has led to a rich ethical tradition that provides a solid foundation for spiritual practice, offering guidance on how to live a life of integrity, compassion, and wisdom.

The significance of the Yamas and Niyamas in yoga philosophy

The significance of the Yamas and Niyamas in yoga philosophy is particularly noteworthy, as these ethical guidelines form the basis of the eight-limbed path of yoga outlined by Patanjali in the Yoga Sutras. The Yamas, or moral restraints, consist of five principles that guide practitioners on how to interact with the world and others, including nonviolence (ahimsa), truthfulness (satya), non-stealing (asteya), moderation in sensual pleasures (brahmacharya), and non-attachment to possessions (aparigraha). The Niyamas, or observances, are five personal practices that promote self-discipline and spiritual growth, including cleanliness (saucha), contentment (santosha), disciplined effort (tapas), self-study (svadhyaya), and surrender to the divine (Ishvara pranidhana).

These ethical principles serve as a practical guide for yogic practitioners, helping them cultivate the moral virtues necessary for spiritual development. By adhering to the Yamas and Niyamas, individuals can foster a harmonious relationship with themselves, others, and the world around them, creating a conducive environment for spiritual growth and inner transformation. Furthermore, the practice of the Yamas and Niyamas helps to purify the mind and body, paving the way for the higher stages of yoga, including meditation and the ultimate goal of self-realisation.

The influence of Indian ethical teachings on spiritual practice and personal growth.

The influence of Indian ethical teachings on spiritual practice and personal growth extends beyond the realm of yoga, shaping the lives and practices of countless individuals throughout history. The concept of dharma, or one's duty in life, has played a pivotal role in Hinduism, Buddhism, and Jainism, guiding practitioners in living a life of moral and ethical righteousness. Additionally, the principle of ahimsa (nonviolence) has profoundly impacted the spiritual practices of Buddhists and Jains, who strive to minimise harm to all living beings through their actions, words, and thoughts.

In contemporary spiritual practice, the teachings of Indian philosophy continue to offer valuable insights and guidance on ethical living and personal growth. Many modern seekers draw inspiration from the wisdom of ancient Indian texts, such as the Bhagavad Gita, the Upanishads, and the Yoga Sutras, which provide practical advice on cultivating moral virtues and pursuing a life of purpose and meaning. Through studying and applying these teachings, individuals can develop a deeper understanding of themselves and their place in the world, fostering a greater sense of empathy, compassion, and inner peace.

As the world becomes increasingly interconnected and complex, the ethical teachings of Indian philosophy remain highly relevant, offering timeless guidance on navigating the challenges and opportunities of modern life. By embracing the principles of nonviolence, truthfulness, and self-discipline, individuals can cultivate the inner resources necessary to face adversity and uncertainty with grace and equanimity. Moreover, the emphasis on personal growth and self-realisation in Indian thought can inspire individuals to seek higher levels of consciousness and spiritual development, ultimately contributing to a more harmonious, just, and compassionate world.

In conclusion, the role of ethics and morality in spiritual practice is of central importance in Indian philosophy, with various schools and traditions emphasising the cultivation of moral virtues as a foundation for inner transformation and self-realisation. By studying and applying these ethical teachings, individuals can develop the necessary qualities of mind and heart to embark on the path of spiritual growth, ultimately discovering the true nature of reality and the profound interconnectedness of all life. As modern practitioners continue to explore and integrate the ethical principles of Indian philosophy into their spiritual journeys, they can develop a greater sense of purpose, meaning, and fulfilment.

Furthermore, the ethical teachings of Indian philosophy have the potential to contribute significantly to the broader global discourse on morality, ethics, and spirituality. As humanity faces unprecedented challenges in the 21st century, such as climate change, social inequality, and political unrest, the wisdom and insights offered by Indian thought can serve as valuable resources for developing ethical frameworks and spiritual practices that promote peace, understanding, and cooperation among diverse cultures and communities.

By engaging in meaningful dialogue and collaboration, individuals from different philosophical and spiritual traditions can learn from one another, drawing upon the rich heritage of Indian ethical thought to develop new perspectives and approaches to the challenges of our time. In this way, the ancient wisdom of Indian philosophy can continue to inform and inspire contemporary spiritual practice, fostering a global community of seekers dedicated to the pursuit of truth, beauty, and goodness.

In summary, the role of Indian philosophy in spiritual practice is multi-faceted and profound, encompassing various dimensions of ethical and moral development that can enrich and transform the lives of individuals and communities alike. By exploring and embracing the wisdom of Indian thought, modern practitioners can cultivate a deeper understanding of themselves, their relationships with others, and the world around them, ultimately fostering a more compassionate, harmonious, and enlightened global society.

The Path of Self-Inquiry and Non-Dualism in Indian Philosophy

The path of self-inquiry and non-dualism is central to Indian philosophy, providing a framework for seekers to explore the depths of their inner world and transcend the limitations of ordinary perception. By delving into the mysteries of the self and the nature of reality, individuals can gain profound insights and achieve a state of self-realisation, wherein the illusory boundaries between the individual and the ultimate reality dissolve.

The significance of self-inquiry in the quest for self-realisation

Self-inquiry, or atma-vichara, is a cornerstone of Indian spiritual practice, offering a powerful and direct method for understanding the true nature of the self. By turning the attention inward and relentlessly questioning the nature of one's existence, practitioners of self-inquiry can strip away the layers of illusion and ignorance that obscure the true nature of the self, ultimately revealing the ever-present, unchanging reality that lies beneath the surface of everyday experience.

This process of self-inquiry has its roots in the Upanishads, the ancient Indian texts that form the basis of much of Hindu philosophy. The Upanishads emphasise the importance of direct, experiential knowledge in pursuing self-realisation, encouraging seekers to look within themselves to uncover the essence of their being. Through this practice, one can recognise the ultimate truth of their existence, transcending the limitations of the individual ego and realising their true, divine nature.

The teachings of Advaita Vedanta and the non-dual nature of reality

Advaita Vedanta is a prominent school of Indian philosophy that builds upon the teachings of the Upanishads, emphasising the non-dual nature of reality. According to Advaita Vedanta, the ultimate reality, or Brahman, is the unchanging, infinite, eternal consciousness that pervades all existence. The individual self, or Atman, is not separate from Brahman but is, in fact, the same. This realisation of the unity of Atman and Brahman is the ultimate goal of spiritual practice in Advaita Vedanta.

The teachings of Advaita Vedanta, as expounded by the great philosopher Adi Shankara, emphasise that the world of appearances, or Maya, is an illusory construct obscuring reality's true nature. By engaging in self-inquiry and deep contemplation, practitioners can pierce the veil of Maya and come to the direct experience of non-duality, wherein the distinctions between the individual self, the world, and the ultimate reality collapse into a single, unified whole.

The impact of non-dualistic thought on spiritual practice and understanding

The non-dualistic perspective of Advaita Vedanta has profoundly impacted spiritual practice and understanding, both within India and beyond. By offering a direct path to self-realisation, non-dualism has provided countless seekers with a powerful framework for transcending the limitations of the ego and realising their true, divine nature.

The teachings of non-dualism have also influenced the development of other spiritual traditions, both within and outside India. For example, the concept of non-duality has played a significant role in the evolution of Mahayana Buddhism, particularly in the school of Zen, which emphasises the importance of direct, experiential knowledge in the pursuit of enlightenment.

Furthermore, the teachings of non-dualism have resonated with many contemporary spiritual seekers, who are drawn to the simplicity and directness of the self-inquiry process. As a result, non-dualistic thought continues to inspire and inform spiritual practice across diverse traditions and cultures, helping individuals to recognise and embrace the inherent unity that underlies all existence.

The Integration of Indian Philosophy in Modern Spiritual Practice

The resurgence of interest in Indian spiritual practices in the contemporary world

In the contemporary world, there has been a significant resurgence of interest in Indian spiritual practices as people from diverse cultures and backgrounds seek deeper meaning and purpose. This renewed interest can be attributed to several factors, including globalisation, which has facilitated the exchange of ideas and philosophies across borders, and the increasing recognition of the value of ancient wisdom in addressing modern challenges.

Moreover, the stress and dissatisfaction that often accompany the fast-paced, materialistic lifestyle of the modern world have led many individuals to explore alternative paths to happiness and fulfilment. Indian spiritual practices, emphasising inner transformation and self-realisation, offer a compelling alternative to the superficial gratification that dominates much of contemporary life.

The adaptation and incorporation of Indian philosophical concepts in various spiritual traditions

As interest in Indian spiritual practices has grown, so has the adaptation and incorporation of Indian philosophical concepts into various spiritual traditions. Many contemporary spiritual teachers and practitioners have drawn inspiration from the diverse schools of Indian thought, synthesising and integrating these ideas into their teachings and practices.

For example, mindfulness, which has its roots in Buddhist meditation techniques, has gained widespread acceptance in the Western world, both as a secular practice for stress reduction and as a spiritual path for personal growth. Similarly, the teachings of yoga have been embraced by millions of people worldwide, not only for their physical benefits but also for their ability to promote mental clarity, emotional balance, and spiritual insight.

Additionally, the principles of non-dualism, as expounded in Advaita Vedanta, have found resonance in contemporary spiritual movements such as Neo-Advaita and nondual spirituality, which emphasise the direct experience of oneness and the dissolution of the separate self.

The potential for Indian thought to contribute to holistic well-being and personal transformation.

Indian philosophy and spiritual practices have much to offer in promoting holistic well-being and personal transformation. These ancient teachings address the various dimensions of human experience, including life's physical, mental, emotional, and spiritual aspects, providing a comprehensive framework for self-exploration and growth.

In the realm of physical well-being, practices such as yoga and Ayurveda can help cultivate balance, flexibility, and strength while promoting overall health and vitality. Meditation and mindfulness practices can support mental well-being, enhancing self-awareness, concentration, and emotional resilience.

Emotionally, Indian spiritual practices often emphasise cultivating virtues such as compassion, selflessness, and devotion, which can contribute to healthy relationships and a sense of interconnectedness with others. Spiritually, the diverse paths of Indian philosophy encourage individuals to explore the depths of their consciousness, seeking to realise their true nature and transcend the limitations of the ego.

Furthermore, Indian spiritual practices can help individuals navigate the challenges and uncertainties of modern life with greater grace and equanimity. Individuals can develop the resilience and adaptability needed to thrive in a rapidly changing world by cultivating inner resources such as mindfulness, self-awareness, and emotional intelligence.

In conclusion, integrating Indian philosophy and spiritual practice into modern life holds tremendous potential for promoting holistic well-being and personal transformation. As more people worldwide recognise the value of these ancient teachings, the timeless wisdom of Indian philosophy can continue to inspire, guide, and support individuals on their journey toward greater self-realisation and a more harmonious, fulfilling existence.

Conclusion

The deep connection between Indian philosophy and spiritual practice

Throughout the history of Indian philosophy, there has been a profound connection between intellectual inquiry and spiritual practice. The various philosophical schools that have emerged within the Indian subcontinent have all sought to address fundamental questions about the nature of reality, the purpose of life, and the path to self-realisation. In this pursuit, the sages and thinkers of India have developed a rich and diverse array of spiritual practices designed to facilitate inner transformation and awaken individuals to their true nature.

This deep connection between philosophy and spiritual practice can be seen across the wide spectrum of Indian thought, from the metaphysical insights of the Upanishads and the ethical teachings of the Bhagavad Gita to the meditative techniques of Buddhism and the devotional practices of the Bhakti movement. In these traditions, the philosophical concepts serve as a foundation for the practical methods of spiritual growth, providing a coherent and holistic framework for self-discovery and self-realisation.

The richness and diversity of Indian spiritual traditions

The spiritual traditions of India are remarkable for their richness and diversity, reflecting the myriad ways human beings have sought to explore and understand the mysteries of existence. From the ascetic's rigorous self-discipline to the poet-saints ecstatic love, India's spiritual landscape encompasses many practices and perspectives, all aimed at the ultimate goal of liberation and enlightenment.

This diversity is evident in the variety of philosophical schools and the wide array of practices that have emerged within each tradition. For instance, practitioners may choose from various paths within the context of yoga, such as Raja Yoga, Bhakti Yoga, Karma Yoga, or Jnana Yoga, each offering a unique approach to spiritual growth tailored to the individual's temperament and inclinations. Similarly, the Buddhist tradition encompasses a diverse range of practices, from the mindfulness techniques of Theravada Buddhism to the complex visualisations and deity yoga of Vajrayana.

The potential for Indian philosophical ideas to inspire and guide contemporary spiritual seekers

In today's world, the timeless wisdom of Indian philosophy continues to inspire and guide spiritual seekers from diverse backgrounds and cultures. The universal relevance and applicability of these ancient teachings make them uniquely suited to addressing the challenges and opportunities of contemporary life.

As more people around the world turn to Indian spiritual practices in search of greater meaning, purpose, and well-being, the philosophical ideas that underpin these practices can serve as a vital source of inspiration and guidance. By exploring the rich tapestry of Indian thought, contemporary seekers can access a vast repository of wisdom, insights, and practical techniques to support their journey of self-discovery and spiritual growth.

Moreover, the pluralistic and inclusive nature of Indian philosophy offers a model for how different spiritual traditions can coexist and enrich one another in a globalised world. By embracing the diversity of Indian thought and recognising the underlying unity that connects all spiritual paths, individuals can cultivate a more expansive, tolerant, and compassionate understanding of the human quest for self-realisation.

In conclusion, the deep connection between Indian philosophy and spiritual practice reveals the richness and diversity of India's intellectual and spiritual heritage. By exploring the philosophical schools and their associated practices, contemporary spiritual seekers can access a wealth of wisdom, insights, and techniques to support their journey of self-discovery and personal transformation. As interest in Indian spiritual practices continues to grow worldwide, the timeless teachings of these ancient traditions hold the potential to inspire and guide individuals from all walks of life, fostering greater understanding, compassion, and holistic well-being in an increasingly interconnected world.

The Contemporary Relevance of Indian Philosophy

Introduction to the Contemporary Relevance of Indian Philosophy

The resurgence of interest in Indian thought in the modern world

In recent years, there has been a growing interest in Indian philosophy, both in academic circles and among the general public. This resurgence can be attributed to several factors, including increased global connectivity, a desire to explore alternative perspectives, and a recognition of the value of ancient wisdom in addressing contemporary challenges. As we face an increasingly complex and interconnected world, the insights offered by Indian philosophical traditions can provide a fresh perspective and help us navigate the complexities of modern life.

One reason for the renewed interest in Indian philosophy is the recognition that Western philosophical frameworks may not offer all the answers to our most pressing questions. Indian thought, with its rich and diverse traditions, presents a wealth of alternative ideas and approaches that can enrich our understanding of the human experience. Furthermore, the holistic nature of Indian philosophy, which often integrates spiritual, ethical, and scientific dimensions, offers a comprehensive framework for understanding the world and our place in it.

The applicability of Indian philosophical ideas to contemporary challenges

Indian philosophy is of historical and cultural interest and directly relevant to our challenges in the modern world. The diverse schools of Indian thought offer insights and wisdom to help us navigate contemporary issues, from personal well-being and ethical decision-making to environmental conservation and social justice.

One of the key strengths of Indian philosophy is its emphasis on balance, harmony, and interconnectedness. Many of its traditions, such as Advaita Vedanta, Samkhya, and Buddhism, emphasise the fundamental interdependence of all aspects of existence. This perspective can help us cultivate a sense of responsibility for our actions and their consequences for ourselves and the wider world.

Another important contribution of Indian philosophy to contemporary challenges is its focus on inner transformation and self-realisation. Many Indian traditions, such as Yoga and Jainism, offer practical guidance on cultivating mindfulness, ethical conduct, and spiritual growth. These practices can help us develop self-awareness, emotional resilience, and empathy, which are essential for navigating modern life's complexities.

Moreover, Indian philosophy can provide valuable insights into the relationship between humans and the natural world. With its deep appreciation for the interconnectedness of all living beings and its emphasis on nonviolence (ahimsa), Indian thought can inspire us to adopt more sustainable lifestyles and promote environmental stewardship.

In summary, the contemporary relevance of Indian philosophy lies in its ability to offer alternative perspectives and practical wisdom that can help us address the challenges of modern life. By exploring the rich and diverse traditions of Indian thought, we can gain fresh insights into ourselves, our world, and our place in it, ultimately contributing to a more harmonious, just, and sustainable future.

Indian Philosophy and the Environment

The ecological wisdom of Indian philosophical traditions

Indian philosophy has long recognised the intricate connection between humans and the environment. Many of its traditions, such as Hinduism, Buddhism, and Jainism, emphasise the interdependence of all life forms and the responsibility of human beings to live in harmony with nature. This ecological wisdom is deeply embedded in the teachings and practices of Indian philosophical schools, offering valuable insights for addressing contemporary environmental challenges.

For example, the ahimsa (nonviolence) concept in Buddhism and Jainism extends beyond human relationships to encompass all living beings and the natural world. This principle encourages respect for the environment and recognising that our actions affect other life forms. Furthermore, Dharma, central to Hinduism and other Indian philosophies, encompasses the ethical duty to uphold the balance and harmony of the natural world.

The Vedas, ancient Indian scriptures, contain numerous hymns and verses that extol the beauty and sanctity of nature, recognising the divine presence in all aspects of creation. This reverence for nature has given rise to a deep-seated ecological consciousness in Indian philosophical thought, fostering a sense of responsibility for the environment's well-being.

The potential for Indian thought to contribute to sustainable development and environmental conservation.

Indian philosophical traditions offer a wealth of ecological wisdom that can contribute to sustainable development and environmental conservation. By drawing on the insights of these traditions, we can develop more holistic and integrated approaches to environmental management grounded in a profound respect for the interconnectedness of all life.

One key principle that can guide our efforts to promote sustainable development is the concept of moderation and balance, as advocated by many Indian philosophical schools. This principle encourages us to consume resources mindfully and to minimise waste, recognising the limits of the natural world and the need for intergenerational equity.

Another important idea is the emphasis on community and social responsibility in Indian thought. This perspective recognises that environmental conservation is not just an individual concern but a collective responsibility that requires cooperation and collaboration at all levels of society.

Additionally, Indian philosophy's emphasis on inner transformation can help foster a deeper ecological consciousness, motivating individuals to make more sustainable choices and adopt lifestyles harmoniously with nature. By cultivating an awareness of our interconnectedness with the environment, we can see the world as an extension of ourselves and develop a genuine concern for its well-being.

In conclusion, the ecological wisdom of Indian philosophical traditions has much to offer in addressing the environmental challenges of the modern world. By embracing the principles of interconnectedness, balance, and social responsibility, we can develop more sustainable and compassionate approaches to environmental conservation, ultimately contributing to a more harmonious and resilient future for all life on Earth.

CHAPTER NINE

The Global Influence of Indian Philosophy

Introduction to the Global Influence of Indian Philosophy

The historical spread of Indian philosophical ideas

Indian philosophy, with its rich and diverse tapestry of ideas, has had a profound and lasting impact on global intellectual thought and culture. Over the centuries, Indian philosophical ideas have spread beyond the Indian subcontinent, influencing the development of ideas, cultures, and civilisations worldwide. The historical spread of Indian philosophical ideas can be traced through various channels, including trade, the dissemination of religious texts and teachings, and the interaction between scholars and travellers.

One of the earliest and most significant examples of the global influence of Indian philosophy is the spread of Buddhism. Starting in the 3rd century BCE, the Mauryan Emperor Ashoka was pivotal in promoting Buddhism within and beyond his empire's borders. Ashoka sent Buddhist missionaries to various parts of the world, including Sri Lanka, Central Asia, and the Mediterranean. These efforts laid the foundation for the growth of Buddhist communities and the diffusion of Buddhist thought in different parts of the world.

Another significant avenue for the spread of Indian philosophical ideas was trade. The ancient Silk Road, which connected the Indian subcontinent with Central Asia, China, and the Mediterranean world, facilitated the exchange of goods, ideas, and cultural practices. Indian merchants and travellers carried their philosophical ideas and beliefs, contributing to the cross-fertilisation of ideas and enriching global intellectual traditions.

The cross-cultural impact of Indian thought

The cross-cultural impact of Indian thought can be observed in various domains, ranging from religion and philosophy to art, science, and literature. Indian philosophical ideas have left a lasting impression on different cultures, stimulating intellectual discourse and enriching global heritage.

One of the most significant cross-cultural impacts of Indian thought is the influence of Buddhism on East Asian cultures. Buddhism became deeply embedded in the cultural fabric of countries such as China, Korea, and Japan. The teachings of the Buddha were integrated with local beliefs, leading to the development of unique forms of Buddhism, such as Zen in Japan and Pure Land in China. These Buddhist traditions have, in turn, shaped the intellectual, artistic, and social landscapes of these countries.

Indian philosophical ideas have also substantially influenced the development of Greek and Roman thought. The interaction between Indian and Western thinkers during the Hellenistic period and the subsequent exchange of ideas led to the emergence of Greco-Buddhism. This cultural syncretism incorporated elements of Greek and Indian philosophy. The ideas of Indian philosophers, such as reincarnation and the transmigration of souls, found resonance in the works of prominent Greek thinkers like Pythagoras and Plato.

The influence of Indian thought can also be seen in the Islamic world, particularly during the Golden Age of Islam. Indian texts on mathematics, astronomy, and medicine were translated into Arabic and studied by Islamic scholars. The works of Indian mathematicians, such as Aryabhata and Brahmagupta, played a crucial role in shaping the development of mathematics in the Islamic world. Indian ideas on astronomy, such as the concept of the sidereal day, were also incorporated into Islamic astronomy. Moreover, the encounter between Indian and Islamic philosophical traditions contributed to the development of Sufism, a mystical branch of Islam that shares similarities with Indian spiritual practices.

In the modern era, Indian philosophical ideas have continued to capture the imagination of Western intellectuals and spiritual seekers. The 19th and 20th centuries witnessed a renewed interest in Indian philosophy as prominent Western thinkers, such as Ralph Waldo Emerson, Henry David Thoreau, and Aldous Huxley, engaged with Indian texts and ideas. The influence of Indian thought can be seen in various intellectual movements, such as Transcendentalism and the New Age movement, which drew inspiration from Indian spiritual traditions.

The global influence of Indian philosophy is also evident in the popularity of practices like yoga and meditation. These practices, rooted in Indian philosophical traditions, have gained widespread acceptance and have been adapted to suit the needs of diverse cultures worldwide. Today, yoga and meditation are widely recognised for their physical, mental, and spiritual benefits, and they have become an integral part of the global wellness movement.

The cross-cultural impact of Indian thought has also extended to art, architecture, and literature. Indian aesthetics, with its emphasis on the principles of Rasa and Dhvani, has inspired artists and writers across the globe. The distinctive features of Indian art and architecture, such as the intricate temple designs and the use of sacred geometry, have influenced the artistic expressions of other cultures.

In literature, Indian epics like the Mahabharata and the Ramayana have captured the imagination of readers worldwide. These stories have been translated into various languages and have been the basis for numerous adaptations, including plays, movies, and graphic novels. Indian philosophical ideas, such as the concepts of Dharma, Karma, and Moksha, have found their way into global literary discourse, enriching the understanding of the human experience.

In conclusion, the global influence of Indian philosophy is a testament to the richness and depth of Indian thought. The cross-cultural impact of Indian ideas has enriched global intellectual traditions, fostered the exchange of ideas, and contributed to developing a shared human heritage. As the world continues to grapple with contemporary challenges, the wisdom and insights of Indian philosophy offer valuable resources for promoting understanding, tolerance, and cooperation among different cultures and civilisations.

Indian Philosophy and Western Thought

The early encounters between Indian and Western thinkers

The early encounters between Indian and Western thinkers can be traced back to Alexander the Great, who brought Greek philosophers in contact with Indian thinkers during his conquest of the Indian subcontinent. The exchanges between these two intellectual traditions resulted in the mutual influence of ideas and the sharing of knowledge, such as the Indian numeral system, which eventually made its way to Europe through the works of Arab mathematicians.

In the early modern period, European missionaries, traders, and scholars visiting India brought back with them Indian texts and ideas, which were translated and studied by Western scholars. The works of Indian philosophers such as Patanjali, Shankara, and Nagarjuna began to gain attention in the West, sparking interest in Indian thought.

The influence of Indian philosophy on Western intellectual movements, such as Transcendentalism and the New Age

The influence of Indian philosophy on Western intellectual movements became more pronounced in the 19th century when the works of Indian philosophers were translated into European languages and became more widely available. The Transcendentalist movement in the United States, led by figures like Ralph Waldo Emerson and Henry David Thoreau, was deeply influenced by Indian thought, particularly the ideas of the Upanishads and the Bhagavad Gita. These texts were seen as sources of spiritual wisdom that transcended religious boundaries and spoke to universal human concerns. Emerson, for example, incorporated Indian ideas about the unity of all existence and the importance of self-realisation into his writings. At the same time, Thoreau drew on Indian spiritual practices, such as meditation and simplicity, in his classic work "Walden."

In the late 19th and early 20th centuries, the influence of Indian philosophy continued to grow with the emergence of the Theosophical Society and the New Thought movement. These movements incorporated Indian ideas of karma, reincarnation, and spiritual evolution, alongside other Eastern and Western spiritual traditions, in their teachings. Theosophists like Helena Blavatsky and Annie Besant helped popularise Indian thought in the West and facilitated the exchange of ideas between Eastern and Western spiritual traditions.

The New Age movement of the late 20th century, characterised by its eclectic and syncretic approach to spirituality, also drew heavily from Indian philosophy. Ideas like mindfulness, meditation, yoga, and holistic healing became central to New Age spirituality, and Indian gurus and teachers gained prominence in the West, introducing millions to Indian philosophical concepts and practices.

The contributions of Indian philosophy to modern Western thought and spiritual practices

The influence of Indian philosophy on modern Western thought and spiritual practices is multifaceted and widespread. Many contemporary philosophers and thinkers have engaged with Indian ideas directly or indirectly, leading to fruitful exchanges and mutual enrichment.

In psychology, Indian concepts of consciousness, mindfulness, and meditation have been integrated into therapeutic approaches like mindfulness-based cognitive therapy (MBCT) and dialectical behaviour therapy (DBT). These therapies have successfully treated various mental health issues, such as depression, anxiety, and borderline personality disorder. The principles of yoga and meditation have also been embraced by mainstream Western culture to promote physical and mental well-being.

In philosophy, Indian thought has contributed to developing various schools of thought in the West, such as process philosophy, which emphasises the dynamic and interconnected nature of reality, drawing parallels to Indian ideas of interconnectedness and interdependence. Some philosophers, like Ken Wilber, have sought to create integrative frameworks that synthesise insights from Western and Eastern philosophical traditions, including Indian thought, to address the challenges and complexities of the modern world.

Furthermore, Indian philosophy has contributed to interfaith dialogue and understanding, fostering a greater appreciation for the diversity of spiritual traditions and the common ground they share. As a result, many people in the West now have a more inclusive and pluralistic view of religion and spirituality, which embraces the wisdom of Indian thought alongside other traditions.

In conclusion, the influence of Indian philosophy on Western intellectual movements and spiritual practices has been significant and enduring. As more people in the West become acquainted with Indian thought, its ideas continue to resonate and inspire, offering valuable insights for understanding the human condition and addressing contemporary challenges. The ongoing dialogue between Indian philosophy and Western thought is a testament to the richness and relevance of these ancient wisdom traditions, which have much to offer the modern world.

The Global Spread of Indian Spiritual Practices

The international popularity of yoga and meditation

In recent decades, Indian spiritual practices, such as yoga and meditation, have gained immense popularity worldwide. Yoga originated in ancient India and has become a global phenomenon, with millions of practitioners across various countries embracing it for its physical, mental, and spiritual benefits. Today, yoga studios can be found in cities and towns worldwide, and the practice has become an integral part of the global wellness and fitness industry.

Meditation, another spiritual practice with roots in Indian philosophy, has also experienced a surge in the global interest. People of diverse cultural backgrounds have adopted various forms of meditation, such as mindfulness, transcendental meditation, and loving-kindness meditation. Scientific research has demonstrated the numerous health benefits of regular meditation, including stress reduction, improved focus, and enhanced emotional well-being. As a result, meditation has been incorporated into various professional and educational settings, with companies and schools offering meditation sessions to promote mental health and productivity.

The cross-cultural adaptation of Indian spiritual techniques

As Indian spiritual practices like yoga and meditation have spread across the globe, they have been adapted and modified to suit the needs and preferences of diverse populations. For example, various styles of yoga have emerged, such as Hatha, Vinyasa, and Ashtanga, each offering a unique approach to the practice. Similarly, meditation techniques have been customised to cater to different goals and preferences, with guided, silent, and group meditation sessions becoming increasingly popular.

The adaptation of Indian spiritual techniques has also led to the development of new practices that blend Indian traditions with other cultural influences. For instance, Western psychology has integrated mindfulness meditation into therapeutic interventions, such as Mindfulness-Based Stress Reduction (MBSR) and Mindfulness-Based Cognitive Therapy (MBCT). These approaches have effectively combined ancient Indian wisdom with modern psychological understanding to address mental health issues and promote overall well-being.

The impact of Indian spiritual practices on global well-being and mental health

The spread of Indian spiritual practices has profoundly impacted individuals' and communities' well-being and mental health worldwide. Yoga has been shown to improve physical fitness, flexibility, and strength while also promoting relaxation and stress reduction. With its numerous scientifically proven benefits, meditation has become a widely recognised tool for managing stress, anxiety, and depression and fostering emotional balance and resilience.

In addition to their benefits, Indian spiritual practices have contributed to the broader global movement towards holistic health and wellness. This movement recognises the interconnectedness of physical, mental, and emotional health and encourages individuals to adopt a more balanced and integrated approach to their well-being. By incorporating Indian spiritual practices into their daily lives, people from various cultural backgrounds have been able to experience the transformative power of these ancient techniques and improve their overall quality of life.

In conclusion, the global influence of Indian spiritual practices, such as yoga and meditation, has been significant and far-reaching. Their widespread popularity and cross-cultural adaptation have led to the development of new practices and therapeutic interventions that have positively impacted the lives of millions of people worldwide. As these practices continue to gain traction and evolve, they will undoubtedly continue to contribute to the global well-being and mental health of individuals and communities.

The global influence of Indian spiritual practices reflects the timeless wisdom and appeal of Indian philosophical ideas. By transcending cultural and geographical boundaries, these practices have enriched people's lives worldwide, fostering personal growth, inner peace, and holistic well-being. As humanity faces the challenges of the modern world, the ancient wisdom of Indian philosophy and spirituality will continue to serve as a guiding light, inspiring individuals to lead more balanced, harmonious, and fulfilling lives.

Indian Philosophy and Eastern Thought

The historical connections between Indian, Chinese, and Japanese philosophical traditions

The profound connections between Indian, Chinese, and Japanese philosophical traditions have shaped the intellectual landscape of Asia for millennia. The spread of Indian ideas to East Asia was facilitated by cultural exchanges, trade, and the transmission of religious teachings, particularly Buddhism. As Buddhism gained popularity in China and Japan, it served as a vehicle for introducing and disseminating Indian philosophical ideas.

Indian thought, particularly the concepts of karma, rebirth, and the pursuit of spiritual liberation, significantly influenced Chinese and Japanese philosophical systems. Moreover, Chinese and Japanese thinkers often engaged with Indian ideas, developing new philosophical perspectives and schools incorporating Indian insights.

The influence of Indian philosophy on the development of East Asian spiritual practices and beliefs

Indian philosophy has profoundly impacted the development of East Asian spiritual practices and beliefs. The teachings of Buddhism, which originated in India, have been particularly influential in shaping the religious and spiritual landscape of China, Japan, and other East Asian countries.

Buddhist ideas and practices were often blended with local religious beliefs and customs, resulting in unique forms of East Asian Buddhism that incorporated elements of Indian thought. For instance, the Chinese schools of Chan (Zen) Buddhism and Pure Land Buddhism have roots in Indian Mahayana Buddhism but have evolved into distinct traditions in their own right.

The mutual exchange of ideas and concepts between Indian and Eastern philosophical schools

The exchange of ideas and concepts between Indian and Eastern philosophical schools has not been a one-way street. While Indian philosophy has undoubtedly influenced Chinese and Japanese thought, these Eastern traditions have also contributed to developing and refining Indian philosophical ideas.

For example, the interaction between Indian Buddhist scholars and their Chinese counterparts led to new schools of Buddhist thought, such as the Yogacara and Madhyamaka. These developments not only enriched the Indian Buddhist tradition but also contributed to the diversity of Buddhist thought in East Asia.

Similarly, the influence of Daoism and Confucianism on Indian thought can be observed in the syncretic development of various philosophical and religious ideas. Blending Indian and Chinese concepts led to unique schools of thought that combined elements of both traditions. For instance, integrating Daoist principles into Indian Tantric practices resulted in the development of distinctive forms of Tantra in both China and Japan.

In conclusion, the historical connections between Indian, Chinese, and Japanese philosophical traditions have resulted in a dynamic and mutually enriching exchange of ideas and concepts. This cross-cultural interaction has shaped Asia's intellectual and spiritual landscape and contributed to the global diversity of philosophical thought. As we continue to explore the global influence of Indian philosophy, it is essential to recognise the deep interconnectedness of Eastern intellectual traditions and how they have influenced and enriched one another.

The Role of Indian Philosophy in Interfaith Dialogue

The shared philosophical concepts and values across religious traditions

Indian philosophy has significantly promoted interfaith dialogue due to its rich array of shared philosophical concepts and values that resonate across religious traditions. The emphasis on universal values such as compassion, nonviolence, and the pursuit of truth in many Indian philosophical systems has allowed meaningful conversations and exchanges among diverse faiths.

For example, the core teachings of ahimsa (nonviolence) and karuna (compassion) found in Hinduism and Buddhism align with similar values in Christianity, Islam, and Judaism. Likewise, the pursuit of self-realisation and spiritual liberation in Indian thought parallels the mystical traditions of other religions, such as Sufism in Islam and Kabbalah in Judaism.

The potential for Indian thought to foster understanding and collaboration among diverse faiths.

Indian philosophical ideas have the potential to foster understanding and collaboration among diverse faiths by promoting tolerance, mutual respect, and the recognition of shared values. By highlighting the common ground among different religious traditions, Indian philosophy can encourage meaningful dialogue and the exploration of shared spiritual insights.

For instance, religious pluralism in many Indian philosophical traditions emphasises that multiple paths to truth and spiritual growth can coexist. This idea can facilitate a more inclusive and open-minded approach to interfaith dialogue, as it acknowledges the validity and value of diverse religious perspectives. Additionally, the emphasis on spiritual practice and personal transformation in Indian thought can provide a common ground for followers of different faiths to engage in shared spiritual activities, such as meditation and contemplation.

The impact of Indian philosophy on global interfaith initiatives and movements

The impact of Indian philosophy on global interfaith initiatives and movements has been significant. Indian thought has inspired numerous individuals, organisations, and events that promote harmony, understanding, and cooperation among people of diverse faiths.

One notable example is the Parliament of the World's Religions, an international interfaith organisation that aims to cultivate harmony among the world's religious and spiritual communities.

Founded in 1893, the Parliament has held multiple gatherings where representatives from various faiths have come together to discuss shared values, concerns, and aspirations. Indian spiritual leaders and philosophers, such as Swami Vivekananda and Sri Sri Ravi Shankar, have played prominent roles in these gatherings, sharing insights from Indian thought and promoting dialogue among religious traditions.

Another example is the growing interest in mindfulness and meditation practices rooted in Indian philosophical traditions such as Buddhism and Yoga. People from various religious backgrounds have embraced these practices as they recognise the potential for mindfulness and meditation to foster inner peace, personal growth, and a deeper connection with the divine. The popularity of these practices has led to the creation of numerous interfaith meditation centres and retreats, where individuals from different faiths can come together to learn and practice meditation techniques in a supportive and inclusive environment.

Furthermore, Indian philosophy has inspired prominent spiritual figures, such as Mahatma Gandhi and the Dalai Lama, who have championed the cause of interfaith dialogue and understanding. Their teachings and actions have been instrumental in promoting peace, tolerance, and mutual respect among followers of different faiths. They have encouraged people to look beyond their differences and recognise the shared spiritual and ethical values that unite them.

In recent years, there has also been a growing interest in studying and applying Indian philosophical concepts in psychology, neuroscience, and well-being. This interdisciplinary engagement has further highlighted the universal relevance and applicability of Indian thought, providing new avenues for interfaith dialogue and collaboration.

In conclusion, Indian philosophy, emphasising universal values, spiritual practice, and religious pluralism, has fostered interfaith dialogue and understanding among diverse religious traditions. Its impact on global interfaith initiatives and movements has been significant, inspiring individuals and organisations to work together to pursue harmony, cooperation, and the exploration of shared spiritual insights. By continuing to engage with and draw inspiration from Indian philosophical ideas, we can further enrich the global tapestry of interfaith dialogue and contribute to a more inclusive, tolerant, and peaceful world.

Indian Philosophy in Contemporary Global Arts and Culture

The influence of Indian aesthetics on world arts and literature

Indian philosophy has profoundly impacted global arts and literature, with its aesthetics, themes, and symbolism deeply influencing various art forms worldwide. Indian aesthetics, such as rasa (emotional essence) and dhvani (suggested meaning), have shaped the artistic expressions in poetry, drama, and visual arts within India and beyond.

For instance, the works of famous poets and writers such as Rabindranath Tagore, Rumi, and William Butler Yeats reflect the influence of Indian thought on world literature. These authors and countless others have drawn inspiration from Indian philosophical concepts, incorporating them into their creative works and exploring the depths of human emotions, experiences, and the nature of reality.

The incorporation of Indian philosophical themes in contemporary art, film, and music

Indian philosophical themes have found their way into various contemporary art forms, including film, music, and visual arts. Exploring Indian thought in these artistic expressions has contributed to a richer, more diverse global cultural landscape.

In contemporary cinema, Indian philosophical themes have been explored in films such as "The Matrix," which delves into the nature of reality and illusion, drawing parallels with the Hindu concept of Maya. Similarly, the critically acclaimed film "Groundhog Day" can be seen as an exploration of the ideas of karma and rebirth. Bollywood films, too, often incorporate philosophical themes, weaving them into narratives that resonate with audiences in India and worldwide.

In music, Indian philosophical ideas have influenced a wide range of artists and genres, from the Beatles' exploration of Indian spirituality in the 1960s to contemporary electronic and ambient music that incorporates Indian instruments and themes. The fusion of Indian classical music with Western genres has created unique and innovative musical expressions that continue to captivate global audiences.

In visual arts, Indian philosophical concepts have inspired contemporary artists to explore themes of identity, the nature of reality, and the interconnection of all beings. The use of Indian symbolism, motifs, and sacred geometry in modern art has produced thought-provoking and visually stunning works that reflect the depth and richness of Indian thought.

The global appeal of Indian cultural expressions rooted in philosophical thought

The global appeal of Indian cultural expressions rooted in philosophical thought can be attributed to the universality of the ideas and values that underpin these expressions. Indian philosophy explores fundamental questions about the human condition, the nature of existence, and the pursuit of spiritual growth, which resonate with people from diverse cultural backgrounds.

Moreover, Indian thought encourages the exploration of diverse perspectives and the celebration of plurality, making it particularly well-suited to the global stage. As a result, Indian cultural expressions that draw upon philosophical ideas have the potential to foster cross-cultural understanding, appreciation, and dialogue.

In today's interconnected world, the influence of Indian philosophy on global arts and culture serves as a testament to the power of ideas to transcend borders and unite people. By continuing to engage with Indian philosophical thought and incorporating its insights into contemporary artistic expressions, we can create a richer, more diverse, and harmonious global cultural landscape.

The Role of Indian Philosophy in Addressing Global Challenges

The potential for Indian philosophical ideas to contribute to sustainable development and environmental conservation

Indian philosophical traditions, with their deep-rooted respect for the environment and the interconnectedness of all life forms, offer valuable insights that can contribute to sustainable development and environmental conservation. Concepts such as Ahimsa (nonviolence) and the idea that the Earth is a nurturing mother (Dharti Mata) can help promote a more conscientious and compassionate approach to our relationship with the planet.

The principles of balance, harmony, and interdependence found in Indian thought can guide us towards a more holistic and sustainable approach to development that prioritises the well-being of all living beings and ecosystems. By drawing on the ecological wisdom of Indian philosophy, we can work towards creating a more sustainable and environmentally responsible global society.

The relevance of Indian ethical and moral principles in tackling social and political issues

Indian ethical and moral principles provide a strong foundation for addressing social and political challenges in today's world. The ideas of Dharma (righteous duty), Karma (the law of cause and effect), and the pursuit of the four Purusharthas (the four goals of human life – Dharma, Artha, Kama, and Moksha) provide a framework for individuals and societies to make morally sound choices that prioritise the well-being of all.

The emphasis on social justice and equality in Indian thought can help guide contemporary efforts to address poverty, discrimination, and social exclusion. By promoting values such as compassion and empathy and recognising the innate dignity of all beings, Indian ethical principles can contribute to developing more inclusive and equitable societies.

The application of Indian philosophical concepts to modern scientific and technological challenges

Indian philosophical concepts can also be applied to modern scientific and technological challenges. The emphasis on the interconnectedness of all things in Indian thought can inspire more holistic approaches to scientific research and technological innovation, considering discoveries' immediate benefits, long-term consequences, and broader implications.

The Indian tradition of scepticism and the importance placed on logical reasoning can contribute to more rigorous scientific inquiry and the development of ethical guidelines for emerging technologies. For instance, the principles of Ahimsa and the pursuit of knowledge for the greater good can inform debates around the ethical use of artificial intelligence and genetic engineering, helping to ensure that these technologies are employed responsibly and for the benefit of all.

Furthermore, Indian philosophy's focus on integrating different forms of knowledge, from empirical observation to introspective contemplation, can encourage interdisciplinary approaches to problem-solving in science and technology. By drawing on the insights and methodologies of Indian thought, researchers and innovators can potentially develop novel solutions to pressing global challenges.

In conclusion, Indian philosophical ideas have much to offer in addressing contemporary issues, from sustainable development and environmental conservation to social justice and technological innovation. Engaging with these rich and diverse traditions can gain valuable insights and perspectives to create a more just, compassionate, and sustainable world. The global influence of Indian philosophy is a testament to its enduring relevance and potential to inspire new ways of thinking and acting in the 21st century and beyond.

Indian Philosophy in the Global Intellectual Discourse

The increasing recognition of Indian philosophical contributions in academic circles

In recent years, there has been a growing interest in and recognition of Indian philosophical contributions within academic circles. Scholars and researchers from various disciplines increasingly engage with Indian thought, recognising its potential to enrich our understanding of the human experience and offer valuable insights into various subjects. This renewed interest has led to the publication of numerous books, articles, and academic courses devoted to the study of Indian philosophy, both in India and around the world.

The inclusion of Indian philosophy in the global intellectual discourse acknowledges its rich history and the depth of its ideas, which span thousands of years and encompass diverse traditions and perspectives. As more people become aware of the profound wisdom contained within Indian philosophical texts, the influence of Indian thought will likely continue to grow in academic settings and beyond.

The potential for Indian thought to enrich and expand global philosophical discussions.

Indian philosophy has much to offer regarding enriching and expanding global philosophical discussions. Its diverse traditions and perspectives provide a wealth of knowledge and wisdom that can contribute to our understanding of the human condition, our place in the universe, and the nature of reality.

By engaging with Indian philosophical ideas, contemporary thinkers can encounter novel concepts and frameworks that challenge conventional wisdom and provoke new ways of thinking. For example, the non-dualistic perspective of Advaita Vedanta invites us to reconsider the nature of the self and the world. At the same time, the ethical principles of Jainism encourage a deep reflection on the interconnectedness of all beings and the importance of nonviolence and compassion. Furthermore, the holistic approach of Indian philosophy, which often integrates diverse aspects of human experiences, such as ethics, aesthetics, and spiritual practice, can inspire interdisciplinary discussions and collaborations across different fields of study.

Incorporating Indian philosophical perspectives into global intellectual discourse can also facilitate a more inclusive and pluralistic understanding of the world, helping to bridge cultural divides and promote dialogue among people of diverse backgrounds and beliefs. By embracing the wide variety of philosophical traditions worldwide, we can cultivate a more comprehensive and nuanced appreciation of the human experience and the many ways individuals and cultures have sought to make sense of life's mysteries.

The prospects for Indian philosophy in the global intellectual arena

The increasing recognition of Indian philosophy in the global intellectual arena bodes well for its prospects. As more people become familiar with its ideas and engage with its rich traditions, Indian philosophy is poised to make even greater contributions to global philosophical and intellectual discourse.

One way in which Indian philosophy can continue to grow in prominence is through increased collaboration and exchange between scholars and researchers from different cultures and disciplines. By working together and sharing insights, the global intellectual community can benefit from the diverse perspectives and wisdom that Indian philosophy offers.

Additionally, incorporating Indian philosophical concepts and principles into contemporary educational curricula can help to foster a greater appreciation for the richness and depth of Indian thought among future generations. This, in turn, can create a more inclusive and pluralistic intellectual landscape in which the insights and ideas of Indian philosophy are given the recognition and attention they deserve.

In the broader cultural sphere, the growing interest in Indian philosophy can also be seen in the increasing popularity of Indian-inspired arts, literature, and media. This trend suggests that the ideas and values inherent in Indian philosophical traditions are resonating with people from diverse backgrounds and walks of life, further expanding the reach and impact of Indian thought in the global arena.

Finally, the continued exploration of Indian philosophical ideas in the context of contemporary challenges, such as environmental sustainability, social justice, and technological advancements, can demonstrate the enduring relevance and applicability of Indian thought to the pressing issues of our time. By offering fresh perspectives and innovative solutions, Indian philosophy can play a vital role in shaping the future of global intellectual discourse and, ultimately, contribute to the betterment of our world.

In conclusion, the prospects for Indian philosophy in the global intellectual arena are bright. As its ideas and traditions continue to gain recognition and appreciation, Indian philosophy has the potential to make significant contributions to global philosophical discussions, enriching our understanding of the human experience and providing valuable insights to address the challenges of our contemporary world. By embracing the wisdom of Indian thought and engaging in cross-cultural dialogue, we can create a more inclusive, pluralistic, and vibrant intellectual landscape that fosters understanding, collaboration, and progress for all.

Conclusion

The enduring global influence and appeal of Indian philosophy

In conclusion, the enduring global influence and appeal of Indian philosophy can be attributed to its rich heritage, profound insights, and universal relevance. Spanning thousands of years, Indian philosophical traditions have offered a wealth of wisdom that has shaped not only the Indian subcontinent but also the wider world. As interest in Indian thought continues to grow in the modern era, it is evident that these ancient ideas still resonate with people from diverse cultures and backgrounds, underscoring their enduring significance and universal appeal.

The potential for Indian thought to inspire cross-cultural understanding and collaboration

One of the key strengths of Indian philosophy lies in its potential to inspire cross-cultural understanding and collaboration. By embracing tolerance, pluralism, and inclusivity, Indian thought has fostered a spirit of openness and dialogue, enabling it to engage meaningfully with various intellectual and cultural traditions. In a world marked by increasing interconnectedness and interdependence, the ability of Indian philosophy to bridge divides and foster understanding across different cultures is more important than ever. By drawing on the insights of Indian thought, we can promote mutual respect, appreciation, and collaboration among people from diverse backgrounds, thereby contributing to a more harmonious and inclusive global society.

The importance of engaging with Indian philosophy in pursuing global wisdom and knowledge

Furthermore, engaging with Indian philosophy can significantly enrich our pursuit of global wisdom and knowledge. By delving into the vast and varied landscape of Indian philosophical thought, we not only gain access to a treasure trove of insights and ideas but also expand our intellectual horizons and deepen our understanding of the human experience. Studying Indian philosophy

challenges us to question our assumptions, refine our perspectives, and broaden our conceptual frameworks, ultimately leading to a more nuanced and comprehensive grasp of the world around us. By incorporating Indian philosophical ideas into global intellectual discourse, we stand to benefit from a richer and more diverse pool of knowledge, which can, in turn, foster innovation, creativity, and progress across various domains of human inquiry and endeavour.

In addition, as we confront the complex and pressing challenges of the 21st century, the wisdom of Indian philosophy offers valuable guidance and inspiration. From promoting sustainable development and environmental conservation to addressing social and political issues, the ethical and moral principles embedded in Indian thought can provide a solid foundation for crafting effective solutions to today's problems. Moreover, by applying Indian philosophical concepts to modern scientific and technological challenges, we can explore new avenues of inquiry and uncover novel approaches to understanding the world and our place in it.

In conclusion, the global influence and appeal of Indian philosophy are a testament to this ancient intellectual tradition's depth, diversity, and relevance. As we navigate the complexities of the contemporary world, engaging with Indian thought can offer us valuable insights, inspire cross-cultural understanding, and contribute to the ongoing quest for wisdom and knowledge. By continuing to explore and appreciate the rich legacy of Indian philosophy, we can ensure that its timeless ideas continue to enrich our lives and shape our collective future.

Rediscovering and Preserving the Heritage of Indian Philosophy.

Introduction to Rediscovering and Preserving Indian Philosophy

The rich and diverse heritage of Indian philosophy represents a treasure trove of knowledge and wisdom that has shaped the lives of countless generations across millennia. With its profound insights into the nature of existence, the human condition, and the pursuit of spiritual and ethical fulfilment, Indian philosophy has much to offer to contemporary audiences seeking to navigate the complexities of the modern world. As such, the preservation and promotion of Indian philosophical heritage are paramount, not only for safeguarding the cultural legacy of India but also for enriching global intellectual discourse and fostering cross-cultural understanding.

The Importance of Preserving and Promoting Indian Philosophical Heritage

The preservation of Indian philosophical heritage is crucial for several reasons. First, it ensures the continuity of a rich and diverse intellectual tradition that has inspired and guided countless individuals throughout history. By safeguarding the texts, teachings, and practices that comprise Indian philosophy, we can ensure that future generations continue to benefit from the insights and wisdom of these ancient thinkers.

Second, preserving Indian philosophical heritage helps to counteract the erosion of cultural identity and promotes a sense of pride and belonging among the people of India. In a world that is increasingly dominated by homogenising forces and the spread of Western cultural values, preserving India's unique intellectual traditions can help foster a sense of cultural distinctiveness and continuity.

The Contemporary Efforts to Revive and Protect Indian Thought

In recent years, there has been a growing awareness of the importance of preserving and promoting Indian philosophical heritage. This has led to several efforts, both within India and globally, to revive and protect Indian thought.

Digitisation and Preservation of Manuscripts: A significant challenge in preserving Indian philosophical heritage is the fragile state of many ancient manuscripts. Efforts have been made to digitise these manuscripts, allowing them to be preserved and accessible to scholars and researchers worldwide. Institutions such as the National Mission for Manuscripts in India and the Indira Gandhi National Centre for the Arts have played an essential role in this process.

Academic Initiatives: Universities and research institutions in India and abroad have increasingly recognised the importance of Indian philosophy in the global intellectual landscape. This has led to the establishment of academic programs and research centres dedicated to studying Indian philosophical traditions, such as the

Oxford Centre for Hindu Studies and the Indian Council of Philosophical Research.

Public Outreach and Education: There is a growing recognition that preserving Indian philosophical heritage requires broader public engagement and appreciation of its value. Initiatives such as lectures, workshops, and cultural events promoting Indian philosophy have become increasingly common, helping to raise awareness and foster interest in these ancient intellectual traditions.

Revival of Traditional Practices: Another aspect of preserving Indian philosophical heritage involves reviving traditional practices associated with these intellectual traditions. This includes promoting and supporting traditional learning institutions, such as gurukuls and pathshalas, where students can study ancient Indian scriptures and languages. Furthermore, efforts have been made to revive traditional arts, crafts, and performance styles that embody Indian philosophical concepts, ensuring that these practices remain relevant and accessible to contemporary audiences.

International Collaboration: The preservation and promotion of Indian philosophical heritage are not limited to India alone. Collaborative efforts between Indian institutions and organisations in other countries have led to increased interest and engagement with Indian thought. This has resulted in the translation of key texts, the organisation of conferences and seminars, and the establishment of research partnerships that contribute to a deeper understanding and appreciation of Indian philosophy on a global scale.

Government Support: Recognizing the importance of Indian philosophical heritage, the Indian government has also taken steps to support its preservation and promotion. Initiatives such as the establishment of the Ministry of Culture, the inclusion of Indian philosophy in the national education curriculum, and the provision of financial support for research and conservation projects are examples of government commitment to safeguarding and promoting India's intellectual traditions.

In conclusion, the efforts to rediscover and preserve the heritage of Indian philosophy are multi-faceted and involve various stakeholders, from scholars and researchers to government agencies and the general public. By working together, these various actors can help to ensure that the wealth of knowledge and wisdom embodied in Indian philosophical traditions is not lost but continues to inspire and guide individuals in the pursuit of truth, meaning, and personal fulfilment. The contemporary efforts to revive and protect Indian thought to demonstrate a growing appreciation for the value and relevance of this ancient wisdom in addressing the challenges of the modern world. Through these endeavours, Indian philosophy can continue to enrich the global intellectual landscape and foster cross-cultural understanding, dialogue, and collaboration. As we move forward, sustaining and expanding these efforts is essential, ensuring that the rich heritage of Indian philosophy remains accessible and relevant to future generations, both in India and around the world.

The Role of Academia in Rediscovering Indian Philosophy

The inclusion of Indian philosophy in academic curricula and research

Academia plays a significant role in rediscovering Indian philosophy by integrating it into academic curricula and promoting research in the field. Educational institutions worldwide have increasingly recognised the importance of including Indian thought in their curricula, particularly in philosophy, religious studies, and cultural studies programs. This inclusion allows students to gain a broader understanding of the philosophical landscape and appreciate the rich intellectual heritage of India.

By incorporating Indian philosophy into academic programs, universities and colleges foster a deeper appreciation for the diversity and interconnectedness of global philosophical traditions. Furthermore, encouraging research in Indian thought contributes to the ongoing rediscovery of the depth and complexity of Indian philosophical systems, their historical development, and their contemporary relevance.

The establishment of dedicated institutions and centres for the study of Indian thought

To facilitate the study and research of Indian philosophy, various dedicated institutions and centres have been established, both in India and internationally. These institutions focus on preserving, promoting, and disseminating knowledge about Indian philosophical traditions by organising seminars, workshops, and conferences and providing resources such as libraries, archives, and digital databases.

In addition to traditional academic institutions, non-profit organisations and cultural centres have emerged dedicated to promoting and preserving Indian philosophy. These centres work to raise awareness about the richness and diversity of Indian thought, engage in intercultural and interfaith dialogue, and foster collaborations between scholars and practitioners from diverse backgrounds.

The contributions of Indian and international scholars to the rediscovery of Indian philosophy

Indian and international scholars have made significant contributions to the rediscovery of Indian philosophy, showcasing its relevance and applicability in the contemporary world. Indian scholars, deeply rooted in their cultural and intellectual heritage, have played a crucial role in interpreting and presenting Indian philosophical systems. They have also worked to bridge the gap between traditional knowledge and modern academic methodologies, ensuring that Indian thought remains accessible and relevant in the global intellectual discourse.

International scholars, too, have contributed to the rediscovery of Indian philosophy by engaging with Indian thought from diverse perspectives and backgrounds. Their efforts have helped to expand the global understanding of Indian philosophical ideas and foster cross-cultural dialogue. These scholars have not only translated and interpreted classical Indian texts but also examined the influence of Indian thought on other philosophical traditions and its potential to address contemporary challenges.

The collective efforts of Indian and international scholars have been instrumental in the ongoing rediscovery of Indian philosophy. Through their research, publications, and teaching, they have brought to light the richness and depth of Indian thought, showcasing its relevance and applicability to various facets of the human experience. This scholarly engagement with Indian philosophy has ensured that its intellectual heritage continues to inspire and enrich global philosophical discourse, fostering a deeper understanding of the diversity and interconnectedness of human thought.

The Digitisation and Preservation of Indian Philosophical Texts

The importance of preserving ancient manuscripts and texts

Preserving ancient manuscripts and texts is paramount in safeguarding the intellectual and cultural heritage of Indian philosophy. These texts form the bedrock of Indian thought, containing invaluable insights and wisdom accumulated over centuries. Ensuring their preservation not only guarantees the continuation of the rich Indian intellectual tradition but also fosters a deeper understanding of the human experience and the development of knowledge across time and space.

The efforts to digitise and make accessible Indian philosophical resources

Efforts to digitise and make accessible Indian philosophical resources have gained momentum in recent years. Digitisation of texts helps preserve and protect them from physical deterioration, loss, or damage, ensuring their availability for future generations. In addition, digitisation makes these resources more accessible to a global audience, allowing scholars, students, and enthusiasts worldwide to engage with Indian philosophical thought. This widespread access to Indian philosophical resources can spark new research, interdisciplinary collaboration, and a deeper appreciation for the diversity and richness of Indian thought.

The role of technology and international collaborations in preserving Indian philosophical heritage

The role of technology in preserving Indian philosophical heritage cannot be overstated. Advanced digitisation techniques, such as high-resolution scanning and optical character recognition (OCR), have facilitated the creation of digital libraries and repositories of ancient manuscripts and texts. Scholars and researchers worldwide can easily access and study these digital resources, fostering a global intellectual dialogue on Indian philosophy.

International collaborations have been crucial in digitising and preserving Indian philosophical texts. Institutions and organisations worldwide have joined forces with their Indian counterparts to preserve and promote India's rich intellectual heritage. These collaborations include sharing technical expertise and financial resources and developing shared digital platforms that host and disseminate Indian philosophical resources.

For instance, the Indira Gandhi National Center for the Arts (IGNCA) in India has partnered with various international institutions to digitise and preserve Indian manuscripts, some of which date back to the early centuries of the Common Era. Similarly, the International Dunhuang Project, a collaborative endeavour involving institutions from multiple countries, has digitised and preserved thousands of ancient manuscripts and texts from the Indian subcontinent, including many works of Indian philosophy. These collaborative efforts highlight the global interest in preserving and promoting the study of Indian thought.

Moreover, private organisations, non-profit entities, and individual scholars have also played a significant role in digitising and preserving Indian philosophical texts. Various open-access platforms, such as the Digital Library of India and the Internet Archive, have made numerous Indian philosophical texts available online for free, facilitating widespread access and engagement with these valuable resources.

In addition to digitisation efforts, preserving Indian philosophical heritage encompasses the oral transmission of knowledge. Many Indian philosophical traditions have been passed down through generations via oral recitation and instruction. Efforts to record and archive these oral traditions help ensure the continuity of Indian philosophical thought in various forms.

Educational initiatives that aim to teach traditional Indian languages, such as Sanskrit, Pali, and Prakrit, also play a crucial role in preserving Indian philosophical heritage. Mastering these languages is essential for engaging with primary source texts and understanding the nuances of Indian philosophical thought. By promoting the study of these languages and supporting the development of linguistic expertise, scholars can continue to explore and analyse Indian philosophical texts in their original form, enriching the global understanding of Indian philosophy.

In conclusion, the preservation and rediscovery of Indian philosophy are essential for fostering a deeper appreciation of India's rich intellectual heritage and its contributions to human thought. Through the use of advanced technology, international collaborations, and a renewed focus on the study of traditional

Indian languages and texts, the global community can ensure the continued availability and accessibility of Indian philosophical resources.

The resurgence of interest in Indian philosophy and the various efforts to preserve and promote its study have the potential to spark new dialogues, interdisciplinary research, and innovative approaches to addressing contemporary challenges. As more scholars and students engage with Indian philosophical thought, the global intellectual community will continue to benefit from the diverse perspectives, wisdom, and insights that Indian philosophy offers.

The revitalisation of Indian philosophy also holds implications for the broader understanding of the human experience, as it showcases the richness and complexity of human thought across cultures and periods. By preserving and promoting the study of Indian philosophy, we contribute to the continued growth and development of global intellectual discourse, ultimately enriching our understanding of the world and ourselves.

Rediscovering and preserving the heritage of Indian philosophy is a task that requires the concerted efforts of individuals, institutions, and governments, both within India and globally. By working together to protect and promote the study of Indian thought, we can ensure that the wisdom and insights of Indian philosophy continue to inspire and guide future generations in their pursuit of knowledge, understanding, and personal growth.

The Revival of Indian Philosophical Languages

The significance of preserving and promoting classical Indian languages, such as Sanskrit, Pali, and Prakrit

Preserving and promoting classical Indian languages such as Sanskrit, Pali, and Prakrit are paramount for the continued study and understanding Indian philosophy. These languages served as the primary vehicles for developing and transmitting Indian philosophical thought, and many seminal texts were written in these languages. By preserving and promoting these languages, we can ensure that these texts' original ideas and concepts remain accessible to contemporary scholars and students.

Furthermore, the revival of Indian philosophical languages can contribute to a richer understanding of the cultural and historical context in which Indian philosophy emerged and developed. Studying these languages can reveal unique insights into how philosophical concepts and debates were shaped by their time's linguistic, cultural, and social contexts.`

The efforts to revitalise the study and use of Indian philosophical languages

In recent years, there has been a growing recognition of the importance of preserving and promoting classical Indian languages. Several initiatives have been undertaken to revitalise the study and use of these languages, both within India and internationally. These efforts include establishing dedicated institutions and academic programs focused on studying Sanskrit, Pali, and Prakrit and developing language learning resources and tools.

The Indian government has also implemented policies to support preserving and promoting these languages, such as establishing the Rashtriya Sanskrit Sansthan, a central institution for studying and promoting Sanskrit. Similarly, the Central Institute of Classical Tamil (CICT) has been set up to promote the study of classical Tamil, another significant language in developing Indian philosophical thought.

In addition to these institutional efforts, there has been a resurgence of interest in learning classical Indian languages among individuals and communities. Online courses, apps, and resources have made it easier for people to access and learn these languages, helping to build a new generation of scholars and enthusiasts who can engage with the rich heritage of Indian philosophy.

The impact of language preservation on the dissemination and understanding of Indian philosophy

The revival of Indian philosophical languages has far-reaching implications for disseminating and understanding Indian philosophy in the contemporary world. As more people learn and engage with these languages, they are better equipped to study and interpret the original texts, leading to deeper and more accurate understandings of Indian philosophical thought.

Moreover, preserving these languages allows for the continued development of new scholarship, translations, and commentaries on Indian philosophical texts. This, in turn, helps to ensure that the rich heritage of Indian philosophy remains accessible and relevant to a global audience. Engaging with the original languages and texts allows contemporary scholars to uncover previously overlooked or misunderstood aspects of Indian thought, leading to new insights and discoveries.

In conclusion, revitalising Indian philosophical languages, such as Sanskrit, Pali, and Prakrit, plays a crucial role in preserving and promoting the heritage of Indian philosophy. Investing in the study and use of these languages ensures that the original ideas and concepts presented in the classical texts remain accessible to future generations of scholars and spiritual seekers. Furthermore, preserving these languages contributes to a deeper understanding of the historical and cultural context in which Indian philosophy emerged and evolved.

The efforts to revive Indian philosophical languages, combined with the growing interest in learning these languages among individuals and communities, have the potential to significantly impact the dissemination and understanding of Indian philosophy in the modern world. As more people engage with the original languages and texts, we can expect to see new scholarship, translations, and interpretations that will further enrich the study of Indian philosophy and its relevance to contemporary challenges and concerns.

The revival of Indian philosophical languages is not just a matter of historic preservation but also an essential step towards ensuring the continued vitality and relevance of Indian philosophy in the global intellectual discourse. By fostering a deeper engagement with the original languages and texts, we can create a more robust and diverse understanding of Indian philosophical thought, contributing to a richer and more nuanced global conversation about the nature of reality, ethics, and the human experience.

Cultural Initiatives and Public Outreach

The role of cultural events and festivals in promoting Indian philosophy

Cultural events and festivals have long been crucial in promoting Indian philosophy. They offer opportunities for individuals and communities to engage with philosophical ideas through various artistic and intellectual mediums. These events often incorporate lectures, panel discussions, workshops, and performances that showcase the rich diversity of Indian philosophical thought, enabling participants to learn about and appreciate the depth and complexity of Indian traditions.

In recent years, there has been a resurgence of interest in organising and participating in cultural events focused on Indian philosophy, both in India and abroad. These events not only serve as a platform for sharing and celebrating Indian philosophical ideas but also provide a means for fostering cross-cultural understanding and dialogue. By bringing together scholars, practitioners, artists, and enthusiasts from diverse backgrounds, cultural events and festivals can facilitate the exchange of ideas and foster an appreciation for the intellectual heritage of Indian philosophy.

The use of modern media platforms to disseminate Indian philosophical ideas

Modern media platforms, including television, radio, podcasts, social media, and digital publications, have become indispensable tools for disseminating Indian philosophical ideas to a broader audience. The increasing accessibility of digital technology has enabled scholars, practitioners, and enthusiasts to share their knowledge and insights about Indian philosophy with individuals worldwide, transcending geographic and cultural boundaries.

These platforms can potentially engage a diverse range of individuals who may not otherwise have the opportunity to learn about Indian philosophy, thereby broadening the scope of its influence and impact. Moreover, modern media platforms can help present Indian philosophical ideas in a manner that is relevant and accessible to contemporary audiences, making it easier for individuals to understand and appreciate the significance of these traditions in their daily lives.

The impact of public outreach and education on the appreciation of Indian thought

Public outreach and education initiatives play a vital role in fostering an appreciation for Indian philosophy, particularly among younger generations who may not have had exposure to these ideas through traditional channels. Such initiatives can take various forms, including workshops, seminars, and online courses introducing the basic concepts, historical context, and contemporary relevance of Indian philosophical thought.

By providing opportunities for individuals to engage with Indian philosophy in a structured and supportive environment, public outreach and education initiatives can facilitate a deeper understanding of the traditions, their underlying principles, and their potential application in various daily life. These efforts can also help to dispel common misconceptions and stereotypes about Indian thought, promoting a more nuanced and accurate perception of the intellectual heritage of India.

In conclusion, promoting and preserving Indian philosophical heritage is essential in today's rapidly changing world. By engaging with Indian philosophy through cultural events, modern media platforms, and public outreach initiatives, individuals can develop a deeper appreciation for the richness and diversity of Indian thought. Through these efforts, the timeless wisdom and insights of Indian philosophy can continue to inspire and guide future generations in their quest for knowledge, understanding, and personal growth.

The Influence of Indian Philosophy on Contemporary Spiritual Movements

The resurgence of interest in Indian spiritual practices, such as yoga and meditation

Over the past few decades, there has been a significant resurgence of interest in Indian spiritual practices, such as yoga and meditation, in various parts of the world. This renewed interest can be attributed to a growing awareness of the benefits of these practices in promoting mental, emotional, and physical well-being. Additionally, the increasing emphasis on holistic health and the search for deeper meaning in life have contributed to the popularity of Indian spiritual practices among people from diverse cultural backgrounds.

Yoga originated in ancient India and has become a global phenomenon, with millions of people regularly practising various disciplines to improve their flexibility, strength, and mental clarity. Similarly, meditation techniques derived from Indian philosophical traditions, such as mindfulness and Vipassana, have gained widespread acceptance as effective tools for stress reduction and personal growth.

The role of Indian philosophical ideas in shaping modern spiritual movements

Indian philosophical ideas have significantly shaped modern spiritual movements in the East and West. The teachings of Indian philosophy, which emphasise the interconnectedness of all beings and the importance of cultivating inner wisdom and self-awareness, have resonated with contemporary seekers looking for alternative approaches to personal growth and self-realisation.

Notable examples of modern spiritual movements influenced by Indian thought include the New Age movement, which incorporates elements of Hinduism, Buddhism, and other Indian spiritual traditions; Transcendental Meditation, which is rooted in the Vedic tradition; and the Integral Yoga movement, which combines the teachings of various Indian philosophical systems, such as Vedanta, Tantra, and Samkhya. These movements have adapted and synthesised Indian philosophical concepts to cater to the needs and sensibilities of a global audience, resulting in the creation of unique spiritual paths that draw upon the rich heritage of Indian thought.

Furthermore, several influential spiritual teachers and thinkers from India, such as Swami Vivekananda, Paramahansa Yogananda, Maharishi Mahesh Yogi, and Jiddu Krishnamurti, have brought Indian philosophical ideas to the forefront of global spiritual discourse. Their teachings have inspired countless individuals to delve deeper into the wisdom of Indian philosophy and adopt its principles in their daily lives.

The potential for Indian thought to contribute to global spiritual development.

The potential for Indian thought to contribute to global spiritual development is immense. It offers a wealth of insights and practices that can facilitate personal transformation, foster a sense of interconnectedness, and promote harmony among diverse cultures and religions. Indian philosophy has much to offer in fostering inner peace, cultivating compassion, and nurturing a reverence for the natural world.

By embracing the principles of Indian philosophy, individuals and communities across the globe can cultivate a deeper understanding of the human condition and the interconnected nature of existence. This understanding can inspire more compassionate, inclusive, and environmentally sustainable ways of living.

In a world faced with myriad challenges, such as social inequality, environmental degradation, and religious strife, Indian philosophical ideas can serve as a source of inspiration and guidance for those seeking to foster global understanding, promote peace, and encourage spiritual growth. By integrating the insights of Indian thought into contemporary spiritual practices and movements, we can create a more compassionate, harmonious, and interconnected global community where diverse spiritual traditions can coexist and learn from one another.

Moreover, the universal principles embedded in Indian philosophical thought, such as the pursuit of self-realisation, the cultivation of inner wisdom, and the recognition of the interconnectedness of all beings, have the potential to resonate with people from diverse cultural backgrounds. This shared spiritual foundation can help bridge the gap between different religions and belief systems, fostering mutual respect, understanding, and collaboration in addressing common challenges.

As we continue to navigate the complexities of the modern world, Indian philosophy can serve as a valuable resource for those seeking a deeper sense of meaning, purpose, and connection. By exploring the rich heritage of Indian thought, contemporary spiritual seekers can discover timeless wisdom that can guide them on their journey towards personal growth, self-realisation, and a more compassionate and interconnected world.

In conclusion, the influence of Indian philosophy on contemporary spiritual movements is both significant and far-reaching. The resurgence of interest in Indian spiritual practices, such as yoga and meditation, combined with the growing awareness of the value of Indian philosophical ideas in addressing contemporary challenges, highlights the continued relevance of this ancient wisdom in the modern world. By preserving, promoting, and integrating Indian thought into global spiritual discourse, we can harness the transformative power of Indian philosophy to inspire personal growth, foster cross-cultural understanding, and contribute to the betterment of humanity as a whole.

The Revival of Traditional Indian Arts and Sciences

The rekindling of interest in classical Indian arts, music, and dance

In recent years, there has been a notable resurgence of interest in classical Indian arts, music, and dance, both within India and worldwide. This revival can be attributed to the growing recognition of these traditional art forms' rich cultural heritage and their intrinsic connection to Indian philosophical thought. Classical Indian dance forms, such as Bharatanatyam, Kathak, and Odissi, are deeply rooted in ancient Indian philosophical and spiritual traditions, often depicting stories and themes from sacred texts like the Ramayana, Mahabharata, and Bhagavad Gita. Similarly, Indian classical music, with its complex melodic and rhythmic structures, is closely linked to the Indian philosophical concept of rasa, or emotional expression, and aims to evoke a profound sense of spiritual transcendence in both the performer and the listener.

The rekindling of interest in these classical art forms is part of a broader movement to preserve and celebrate India's rich cultural heritage while fostering a deeper understanding and appreciation of the philosophical ideas underpinning these artistic expressions. By engaging with traditional Indian arts, music, and dance, audiences can gain a unique insight into the diverse and nuanced world of Indian thought and the profound spiritual principles that have shaped Indian culture for millennia.

The preservation and promotion of traditional Indian sciences, such as Ayurveda and Vastu Shastra

Alongside the revival of classical Indian arts, there has also been a growing interest in traditional Indian sciences, such as Ayurveda and Vastu Shastra. Ayurveda, a holistic system of medicine that originates in the Vedic texts, emphasises the importance of maintaining balance and harmony between the body, mind, and spirit to achieve optimal health and well-being. This ancient science is deeply rooted in Indian philosophical concepts, such as the theory of the five elements (panchabhuta) and the three bodily humours (doshas). It offers a comprehensive understanding of human health that encompasses physical and mental dimensions.

On the other hand, Vastu Shastra is an ancient Indian science of architecture and design that seeks to create harmonious and auspicious living spaces by aligning the built environment with the natural forces of the cosmos. Like Ayurveda, Vastu Shastra is also grounded in Indian philosophical principles, particularly the concept of energy (prana) and the interconnectedness of all things.

The preservation and promotion of these traditional Indian sciences help ensure the survival of valuable knowledge and wisdom passed down through generations and deepen our understanding of the underlying philosophical ideas that inform these practices. Engaging with these ancient sciences can gain valuable insights into reality's holistic and interconnected nature and the importance of maintaining balance and harmony.

The connection between the revival of traditional arts and sciences and the appreciation of Indian

philosophy

The revival of traditional Indian arts, music, dance, and sciences is closely linked to the growing appreciation of Indian philosophy in the contemporary world. As more and more people become aware of India's rich cultural and intellectual heritage, there is a growing desire to engage with and understand the philosophical ideas that have shaped Indian thought and culture for millennia.

The renaissance of traditional Indian arts and sciences provides a unique and accessible entry point into the complex world of Indian philosophy, offering tangible manifestations of the abstract concepts and principles that underlie these disciplines. By engaging with India's artistic and scientific traditions, individuals can gain a deeper understanding of the philosophical ideas that inform these practices and their relevance and applicability to contemporary life.

Moreover, the revival of traditional Indian arts and sciences fosters cross-cultural understanding and dialogue as audiences increasingly embrace and celebrate these practices worldwide. As interest in Indian philosophy grows, we must continue to preserve and promote the rich cultural expressions and intellectual traditions that have shaped the development of Indian thought to ensure that this valuable heritage is not lost to future generations.

The Role of Indian Philosophy in Contemporary Indian Society

The relevance of Indian philosophical ideas in addressing modern social, political, and environmental issues

Indian philosophy has a rich history of exploring complex issues still relevant to modern society. The teachings of Indian philosophy offer valuable insights and guidance in addressing contemporary social, political, and environmental issues. For instance, the concept of Dharma, which emphasises the importance of fulfilling one's duties and responsibilities, can be applied to contemporary concerns such as social justice, equality, and responsible governance.

Ahimsa, the principle of non-violence and respect for all living beings, can provide a solid foundation for addressing environmental issues, promoting sustainable development, and fostering greater compassion and empathy towards the natural world. Similarly, interdependence and interconnectedness, a core of Indian philosophical thought, can help us better understand the complex dynamics of contemporary global issues, such as climate change, economic inequality, and migration.

The potential for Indian thought to contribute to national development and identity

Indian philosophical ideas have the potential to contribute significantly to the development and identity of contemporary Indian society. By drawing upon the rich intellectual and cultural heritage of Indian philosophy, modern Indian society can cultivate a deeper understanding of its historical roots and values, fostering a greater sense of national pride and unity.

At the same time, Indian philosophy can provide a framework for addressing contemporary challenges in areas such as education, healthcare, and social welfare. For instance, the teachings of Indian philosophy can be incorporated into educational curricula, promoting critical thinking, ethical values, and an appreciation for India's diverse cultural heritage. Similarly, the holistic approach to health and well-being found in Indian philosophical traditions, such as Ayurveda, can help shape more effective and sustainable healthcare policies.

Furthermore, by promoting the principles of social harmony, compassion, and tolerance found in Indian philosophy, contemporary Indian society can work towards fostering a more inclusive and equitable social environment. These values can help address discrimination, gender inequality, and communal tensions in some Indian societies.

The influence of Indian philosophy on contemporary Indian culture and values

Indian philosophy continues to shape contemporary Indian culture and values in numerous ways. For instance, the popularity of yoga and meditation is evidence of the enduring appeal of Indian philosophical ideas on health, mindfulness, and spirituality. These practices have been embraced by millions of people around the world, including a growing number of Indians who are rediscovering their cultural heritage.

Additionally, Indian philosophy has influenced modern Indian literature, film, and art, with many contemporary artists and writers drawing inspiration from the rich tapestry of Indian philosophical thought. This can be seen in the works of renowned Indian authors, such as Rabindranath Tagore, who have explored themes related to Indian philosophy in their writings.

The influence of Indian philosophy is also apparent in the everyday values and beliefs of many Indians, who continue to be guided by principles such as Dharma, Karma, and Ahimsa in their personal and professional lives. These values provide a strong ethical foundation that helps individuals navigate the complexities of modern life, fostering a sense of balance, resilience, and inner peace.

In conclusion, Indian philosophy significantly shapes contemporary Indian society, culture, and values. Drawing upon the timeless wisdom of Indian philosophical traditions, contemporary India can address pressing social, political, and environmental challenges while fostering a greater national identity and unity. The influence of Indian philosophy on contemporary Indian culture and values serves as a reminder of the enduring appeal and relevance of these ancient teachings and their potential to guide and inspire future generations.

As India continues to develop and grow globally, the nation's philosophical heritage must be preserved, promoted, and integrated into the fabric of contemporary society. This will not only help India maintain a unique cultural identity but also enable it to contribute meaningfully to global conversations on issues such as sustainability, ethics, and human well-being. By embracing and celebrating the rich heritage of Indian philosophy, contemporary Indian society can forge a path towards a more enlightened, compassionate, and sustainable future.

Conclusion

The importance of rediscovering and preserving the rich heritage of Indian philosophy

In conclusion, the rediscovery and preservation of the rich heritage of Indian philosophy are paramount. The vast corpus of Indian philosophical thought, with its profound wisdom and insights, holds immense potential to guide individuals and societies across the globe towards greater understanding, compassion, and well-being. To harness this potential, concerted efforts must be made to safeguard, study, and share this invaluable treasure trove of knowledge with future generations.

The collective efforts and initiatives that contribute to the revival and promotion of Indian thought

The collective efforts and initiatives contributing to the revival and promotion of Indian thought are varied and multifaceted. These efforts include the establishment of academic institutions, the preservation and digitisation of ancient manuscripts, the promotion of classical Indian languages, the use of modern media platforms, and the inclusion of Indian philosophical ideas in contemporary spiritual movements. Through these endeavours, Indian philosophy finds new life and relevance in today's world, fostering a deeper appreciation of its profound insights and timeless wisdom.

Academic institutions play a pivotal role in rediscovering and promoting Indian philosophy by creating opportunities for rigorous study and research. These institutions and dedicated scholars and researchers help unearth the hidden gems of Indian thought and make them accessible to a broader audience. Moreover, the digitisation and preservation of ancient manuscripts and texts ensure that their knowledge remains available for future generations to study and learn from.

The revival of classical Indian languages, such as Sanskrit, Pali, and Prakrit, is another crucial aspect of preserving Indian philosophical heritage. These languages are the carriers of India's philosophical wisdom, and their preservation and promotion are vital for maintaining the continuity of the country's intellectual traditions. Revising these languages not only supports the dissemination of Indian philosophy but also fosters a deeper understanding of the cultural context in which these ideas were developed.

The potential for Indian philosophy to continue inspiring and guiding individuals and societies across the globe

Cultural initiatives and public outreach efforts significantly bring insights into Indian philosophy to a wider audience. Through events, festivals, and modern media platforms, Indian philosophical ideas are being shared and engaged with by individuals from diverse backgrounds and cultures. This increased accessibility has the potential to inspire countless people worldwide, contributing to global spiritual development and personal growth.

Furthermore, the revival of traditional Indian arts and sciences, such as classical music, dance, Ayurveda, and Vastu Shastra, strengthens the connection between Indian philosophy and the broader cultural landscape. By preserving and promoting these traditional disciplines, a holistic understanding of Indian thought can be fostered, emphasising its relevance and applicability in various spheres of life.

In contemporary Indian society, the relevance of Indian philosophical ideas in addressing modern social, political, and environmental issues cannot be overstated. Indian thought can provide valuable guidance and inspiration for national development and identity and contribute to shaping contemporary Indian culture and values. By engaging with Indian philosophy, individuals and societies can find new ways of navigating the complex challenges of the modern world.

In conclusion, the rediscovery and preservation of the rich heritage of Indian philosophy are crucial endeavours that require the collective efforts of individuals, institutions, and societies. Through these collaborative initiatives, Indian thought can continue to inspire and guide people across the globe, fostering greater understanding, compassion, and harmony among diverse cultures and traditions. The wisdom contained within Indian philosophy has the potential to address many of the challenges faced by contemporary societies, offering guidance on ethical living, sustainable development, and holistic well-being.

By engaging with and preserving the heritage of Indian philosophy, we honour the legacy of India's great thinkers and create opportunities for future generations to learn from and build upon their insights. As the world becomes increasingly interconnected and globalised, the importance of fostering cross-cultural understanding and collaboration has never been more apparent. Indian philosophy emphasises unity, compassion, and the interdependence of all living beings and offers a powerful foundation for such efforts.

The continued exploration and promotion of Indian philosophy in the global intellectual discourse will undoubtedly enrich and expand the world's collective wisdom. By sharing its timeless insights and universal principles, Indian philosophy can contribute to the ongoing pursuit of knowledge and understanding, transcending geographical, cultural, and religious boundaries.

Ultimately, the rediscovery and preservation of the rich heritage of Indian philosophy are essential for perpetuating India's intellectual traditions and for the betterment of humanity as a whole. By embracing the profound wisdom of Indian philosophical thought, we can work towards a future characterised by greater harmony, compassion, and understanding among people from all walks of life.